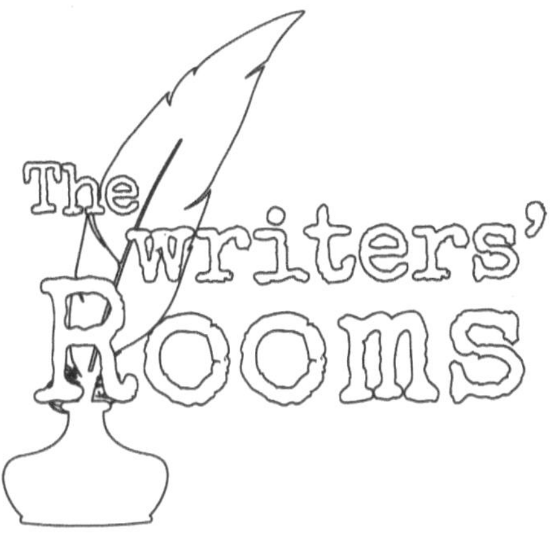

Iowa [W]rites of Winter

A Writers' Rooms Community Anthology

Erin Casey, Jill Cronbaugh, and Nicholas Lee, eds.

First edition, 2024.

The Writers' Rooms

Iowa City, IA

welcome@thewritersrooms.org

Cover art courtesy of Jill Cronbaugh.

ISBN: 979-8-218-44636-9

To the writers of the community who make
The Writers' Rooms possible… thank you.

Table of Contents

Introduction

Dear Reader, thank you for supporting The Writers' Rooms (TWR)! This compilation is our way to celebrate our writers and to thank everyone for helping the Rooms flourish.

Iowa [W]rites of Winter kicks off the new theme in our anthology series.

After publishing four books about the elements, we now turn to the seasons and the rites of passage that come with. We encouraged our writers to think about what winter means to them. In turn, we received a myriad of snowy fairy tales, nostalgic memories, flickering hope, bitter nights and hearts, frigid fiends, and much more. We hope you enjoy them and get swept up in the winter winds.

TWR is an organization which endeavors to create a safe, inclusive community for all writers. We believe that everyone has a wealth of knowledge and a story to share. In our Rooms we bring both to the table. These regular meetings include a myriad of craft discussions, prompts, lessons, and time to socialize and write. Our events, which are usually held in conjunction with local businesses and libraries, offer a safe space in which to meet other members of your local writing community.

Our Rooms would not exist were it not for the incredible writers throughout the creative corridor, as well as our dedicated and brilliant Concierges, the leaders of our Rooms. We've watched new writers learn from seasoned minds. Authors with writer's block have found a way to flourish and venture into their literary world once again. Most importantly, people have found a Room to call home, a place where they feel safe to share their voice and find help when they struggle.

Just remember, no matter where you are in your writing journey, you are never alone. You have a community waiting for you.

Best,

The Publishing Committee

Snow Report

Rachel Schneberger

what if you were a
snowflake
invited,
no longer in droplet form,
out of the sky,
clinging to a dust particle,
vapor freezing,
building new crystals
into six arms
the whole sky
awaiting you
you don't have wings,
you float,
maybe fall,
a silent ballet.

what if you danced down
to the exposed branch
of a tall tree,
use to climb,
your delicate,
not frail, arms
scale
close to the bark,
a shield never offering itself,
you hug, nonetheless.
exposed,
retained,
waiting, accumulating,
wishing
to fall again?

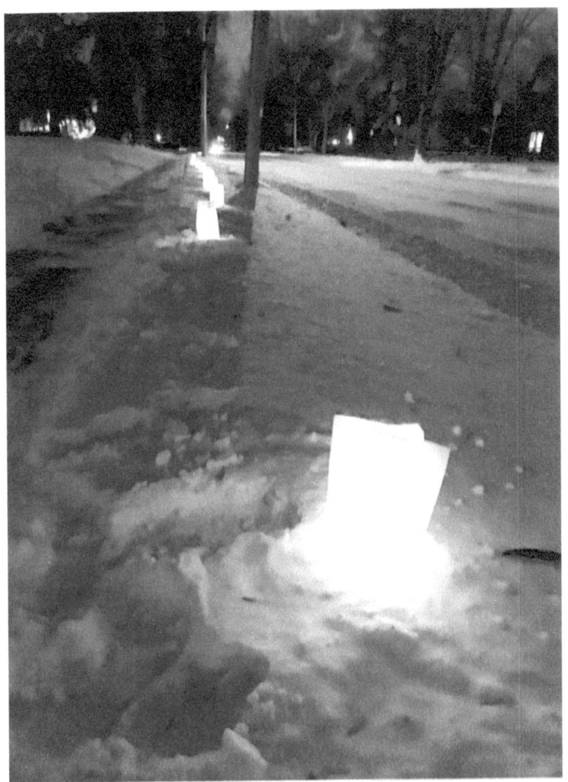

Christmas Eve

Spike Dawkins

Bianca and the Snowy Day

Sharon Falduto

Bianca felt the snow squish over the top of her boot and soak into her sock, then put her other foot into the same drift of snow so that both feet would feel equally cold and wet and no one would feel left out.

Having snow up to her knees was awesome. It had never snowed so much in the whole eight years she had been alive. Usually, it would snow a little bit, maybe some dust on the driveway, and then it would melt. She was pretty sure snow was one of those things that just didn't happen anymore, like people riding horses to school, or having phones that attach to the wall.

She was lucky to even have these boots, even though they were kind of crummy. They were from a cousin, ten years older, from back when it used to snow in Iowa. Her snowpants had one broken strap, held together by a paperclip, from the same cousin. This stuff was just in the basement. Her parents didn't buy snow stuff because it never snowed, so she was glad it was just lying around, and that it mostly fit her.

Bianca swallowed the quiet. No one in the world was talking or making any noise, or if they were, the snow swallowed up all the sound.

Crunch crunch crunch squish wet foot, that was all she heard and felt.

Bianca and the Snowy Day

She loved being outside by herself. Even though she could see the back of her friend Lydia's house from the back of her own house, because their backyards were butt up against each other, this was the first time she had been allowed to walk to Lydia's by herself. Her dad wasn't home, and her mom didn't want to wrap the baby up in all the winter stuff just to take her across two backyards. Bianca was glad to get away from that baby. She figured it would be fun someday, but right now it was just kind of loud.

Bianca's favorite book was "The Snowy Day." She checked it out from the library so many times that her parents finally bought her a copy from the Scholastic book club "Classic" section. For one thing, there was so much snow in that book! It looked like it had snowed six feet in his town! And the little boy in that book got to go outside and play by himself without any parents dragging themselves along to see what he was doing all the time.

Her parents seemed to like that she loved "The Snowy Day." "What is it you like about that book?" her mom asked, and Bianca felt like there was an answer she was supposed to give, but she didn't know what it was. "I like…the snow?" "Okay," Mom said, and Bianca knew that was the wrong answer. "And the little boy? Did you notice anything about that little boy?" "Um…." Bianca already knew that grownups didn't like to hear things like "the little boy gets to play outside with nobody bugging him," so she said, "I like the way his red snowsuit looks on the pages when it's all white with the snow." And her mom said, "Ok," but in a different way, that made it seem like even if it still wasn't quite the right answer, it wasn't the wrong one, either.

Iowa [W]rites of Winter

She wanted to go down a hill like the boy in the story but there weren't any hills between her house and Lydia's, just the piles of snow where it drifted up against the trees. She tried to make a snowball, but the snow was too powdery so that probably meant she and Lydia wouldn't get to build a snowman. Nobody made proper snowmen anymore; they would just be lumps of dirty ugly snow because instead of snow the snowmen were mostly dirt men.

Bianca saw marks in the snow like some kind of animal had left them. She could be a Nature Lady and try to identify the tracks! Deer? No, not big enough. Not paw-y enough to be a dog. Maybe a bunny, with big back feet and little front feet. She tried to see where the tracks led to, but they went away from Lydia's house and she figured she'd better not go too far from the path, since her mother was probably watching through the back window.

Somebody was always watching. Her mom watched her go, and Lydia's mom watched her come. At school the teachers watched. She wanted to have an adventure but she was always never unsupervised. "Unsupervised" was a great word. She heard it from her grandma and rolled it around in her head for a while. It had the word "super" in it, which made it sound good, but then "un," which was the opposite, so maybe it meant un-super? But no, it just meant "nobody watching," which to Bianca was not un-super at all.

"Hey, Bianca!" Lydia hollered out her back door. "Do you want to come in and play?"

"Let's play outside!" Bianca hollered back. "It

Bianca and the Snowy Day

never snows like this!"

"OK, let me find my stuff." In a few minutes, Lydia came out in her winter coat, with just her jeans on and boots that looked way too big. "They're my mom's boots," she said. "What do you want to do? Build a snowman?"

"We can't," Bianca answered. "The snow is too unsticky. But I have an idea. What's your mom doing?"

"I think she's in her closet, sorting stuff."

"Great! My mom is probably done looking at me by now. Let's go follow some tracks."

"Do what?" Lydia asked.

"There's some tracks in the snow, I want to see who they belong to!"

"We can't do that, I'm not allowed to leave my yard."

"UGH," Bianca seethed. "We're not allowed to do ANYTHING! Samantha in American Girl was stopping child labor in factories all by herself at our age! We can't even walk out of our yards. This is stupid, Lydia. I'm going. You wanna come?"

Lydia looked at her house. She looked at Bianca's house. The windows looked like big eyes, staring at the two girls in the snow. But she also saw the white glow of snow reflected in the windows.

"Yes." Lydia decided. "Let's go follow those tracks. But if they go across the street I have to stop, because I'm not allowed to cross the road."

"Ok," Bianca agreed. "There's all these big weird trucks on the road anyway, so let's just stop at the sidewalk."

Bianca and Lydia walked into the neighbor's yard, following the tracks. They mostly didn't step in the animal-left holes. Three backyards over from Lydia's house, the tracks stopped at a tree. "Look!" Bianca pointed, and the girls looked up. A gray squirrel hopped from the branches of one tree to the branches of another. Just when he jumped, snow fell down onto Lydia's face. Bianca and Lydia laughed so hard that they fell over backward. They waved out their arms and legs to make snow angels.

Then they walked back to Lydia's. "That squirrel pooped snow on you!" Bianca shrieked, and Lydia laughed and rolled on the ground getting completely soaked.

A few more steps. "Squirrel poop!" Lydia shouted, and Bianca tried to pick up snow and throw it at her, but it stuck to her mitten instead, and the girls laughed some more.

When they got to Lydia's house, their noses were red and runny, their pants were soaked, and their boots were full of snow. As Bianca pulled her boots off in Lydia's front room she looked her friend in the eyes and said, "Lydia, I think this was the best day of my life."

"Mine too," Lydia whispered. She added, "Maybe next week we can go all the way across the street."

"Right," Bianca said quietly. "And maybe next week…another squirrel will poop on you!"

They both rolled on the floor, tears rolling down their cheeks from laughing.

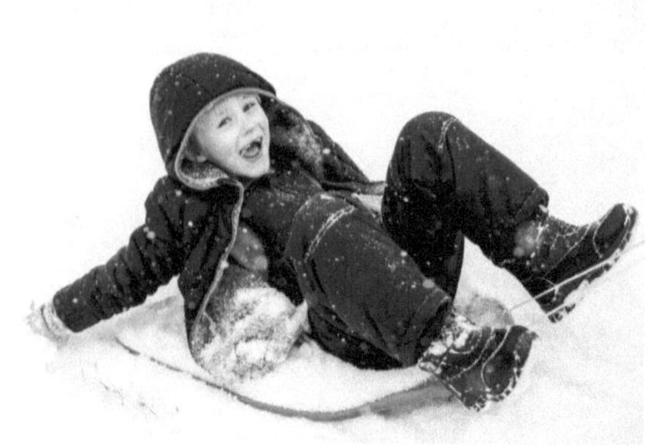

Sledding

Amy Ford

I Am a Snowflake

Sharon Ruth Hensley

I am a snowflake.
Sensitive to the touch,
Well aware I feel too much.

I am a snowflake.
Souls such as mine,
Weren't meant for this time.

I am a snowflake.
Mistakenly seen as meek,
Targeted by those who are weak.

I am a snowflake.
What would our world be,
If there were no one left like me.

I am a snowflake.
Despite damage done,
Somehow I'm still moving on.

I am a snowflake.
Capable of rising above,
Humanity in persistent love.

I am a snowflake.
Authentic and Unique,
Possessing delicate strength.

I am a snowflake.
Naturally gentle and kind,
We need more souls like mine.

If It Didn't Snow in My Town

Rachel Schneberger

Raspberry blooms linger
preserving green tapestry
leaves cease their descent.

Houses forsake the hum,
roofs unsigh 'neath snow's firm hold,
exhalations ease.

Snow plows silent now,
no rumbling around cars,
neighborhoods in peace

The toil in repose,
Silence drapes the rhythmic scrape.
Imagined snowbanks

Snowless town, streets lack
the idyllic hush of flakes

Slipping Down Icy Sidewalks in December

Kelli Brommel

It doesn't matter
That you dread Christmas.
Holidays happen,
Despite your objections.

You walk the mall
Noting every display of
Future landfill fodder,
All the while wishing a fantasy
Monster would crash
Through the skylights,
Jolt people awake
By setting fires or
Crunching bones.
You're oppressed by the heat of
Many bodies milling,
Eyes averted,
No connection
Just being there,
Partly there,
In search of something
A person can't find at the mall.

Holidays mean obligation,
Spending time hanging
With people who have
Nothing good to say
But because you share genes or
Married into a family you
Avoid talking politics and exchange
Things you don't need,
Eat too much to forget,

Iowa [W]rites of Winter

Drink too much to remember.
One day, fewer people to deal with means
Less holiday visiting.
You cramp with guilt,
Because folks dying off
Should cause sadness not relief.

When the kids were small,
You gave half-hearted lessons in the reason
For the season, knowing so
Little yourself.
You'd turn a page each day,
Open paper doors,
Advance the story.
You might have set up
The porcelain crèche
With mended baby Jesus and a
Tacky plastic cow.
Sometimes you miss it-
The ritual,
Not the plastic cow.
Since the kids are adults,
Hunched over screens
Denied to them at six and eight
In lieu of Legos and mindful games,
Is it your job to continue the motions,
The emotions
Of yearly tradition?
You have no will left, can't
Force anyone to do what
You don't want to do yourself.

Stretches of emptiness
Beckon, but
There's little time to sit and be,
To take a walk in the cold,
Get some distance,
Because when you
Slip down icy sidewalks,

Slipping Down Icy Sidewalks in December

Past windows of brightly lit homes,
You'll believe what we all want
To believe
At Christmas,
That the people inside are happy,
That their perfect decorations
Are a sign
They are better at family and holidays,
Better at life.

Sun Prairie

JE Brooke

This is the favorite memory I have of spending time with my grandmother.

***

We hadn't had snow yet that year, and Christmas was coming up. I hugged my mom and dashed out the door to where Grandma was waiting for me in her white minivan in the driveway. She'd agreed to let me go with her up to Sun Prairie to visit her sister-in-law. Ursula was from Germany, and had been married to grandma's brother Rick, who had passed away over the summer. We were going up to Sun Prairie to make sure she didn't feel too alone with the impending holiday, and to see if there was anything that needed to be done around the house that we could do for her. Grandma was always doing that kind of thing for the people she liked; friends, family, grandkids. She found ways of sneaking beanie babies we'd hinted at wanting into our coat pockets, would drive all over town to find us the Happy Meal toy we wanted. Trips to the beach, to the zoo, to get ice cream, to the mall where she'd buy anything I wanted. It seemed perfect. She was a little kid's dream grandparent.

I hadn't found out yet how she could be with people she didn't like.

We took the interstate north. Neither of us had had dinner yet, so we stopped at a McDonald's on the way up. A Bug's Life had just come out in theaters, and in my Happy Meal I got a digital watch shaped like a leaf with the main character's face printed in the center. The outer frame was painted a metallic green and could be attached to a backpack via a carabiner clip. It lived on my backpack for much longer than a toy watch reasonably should have, until the battery finally gave out. I thought about our trip every time I looked at it.

Grandma loved shopping, so we stopped at a mall between the McDonald's and Great-Aunt Ursula's house. The mall was enormous, the halls fully decked for Christmas. Twinkling lights cascaded from the two story-tall ceiling. Festive music pumped through the air. A line to see Santa, enthroned in a red and gold chair -- his display festooned with artificial evergreens and gold ribbons -- snaked around the display toward the food court, ending somewhere around the Cinnabon. I'd already visited Santa that year, so it didn't matter that we were in something of a rush and couldn't wait. We went into the Walden Books instead, even though she didn't really like to read anything other than magazines. Mom had just finished reading Julie of the Wolves to me the night before. I'd hung on every word and cried at all of the really sad parts, so I was thrilled to discover that there was a sequel as Grandma watched me peruse the shelves. We bought the sequel and a couple of other books in series that I was reading, and got back on the road.

Somewhere after we crossed the Wisconsin border, it started to snow in huge, sticky flakes. Grandma had a cassette of old Christmas songs that she put on, and we spent the rest of the drive belting "I want a hippopotamus for Christmas" and "All I want for Christmas is my two front teeth" off-key at the top of our lungs. By the time we pulled into the driveway in Sun Prairie, a couple of inches of snow had accumulated.

It turned out that we weren't the only ones visiting Ursula that evening. Her granddaughter Nina -- who was around my age -- was there as well, so while Grandma and Ursula talked in the living room, Nina and I went outside to play in the snow. I hadn't brought snow pants, only my puffy winter coat, so we made snowmen until my jeans started to soak through. It didn't take long, only about the length of time to roll the base of the snowman. That was just as well. The snowflakes stuck to each other almost too well, and the resulting snowball peeled off the grass in long strips so that it looked more like a rolled-up carpet than a sphere.

Cold and shivering, Nina and I went back inside to sit with Grandma and Ursula in the living room while they talked. I didn't pay much attention to that conversation, sipping hot cocoa and watching An All Dogs Go to Heaven Christmas Carol with Nina on the hulking TV. We stayed for a while, warming up and talking and watching it snow. But it was a school night, and before too long Grandma and I waved goodbye and walked back to the minivan, where we started the journey home through the dark and cold.

***

This is my favorite memory of my grandmother.

It's also one of the few good memories that I have left of her. The intervening years were not kind to our relationship. By the time I was a teenager, she had decided that I was too much like her in all the wrong ways, or not enough like her in all the right ones. Our conversations began to revolve around ways I wasn't living up to my other cousins, or how uninteresting a person I was becoming. I stopped putting in much of an effort to visit with or talk to her. I saw and heard from her less and less until the flow of communication stopped entirely.

I haven't spoken to her in years now, and she's never made the effort to call. I'm not the only person she treats like this, far from it, so it's stopped feeling so personal over the years and more like an inevitability. Still, it's nice to sometimes remember that other version of my grandmother. The mask she wore around me when I was a child, too young to really notice when it slipped in my presence. I keep that memory on a shelf in my mind, and -- when the mood takes me -- I pick it up, give it a shake, and watch the snow fall around us as we drive.

Iced Out

Judith F. Brenner

I slipped off my wedding ring and pushed it into the slit of a small jewelry box that held my rosary and a few pairs of clip earrings. There was the satisfying click shut of the suitcase. I went through the checklist in my head to see what was left, and turned toward the kitchen.

"I'll be right back," I said to Irene, my sister-in-law, a true friend willing to help me and my daughter get away from Joe. I headed downstairs to grab cash hidden in the sewing cabinet. The bottom step wall was scuffed by Joe's belt buckle missing me during that summer fight. I gathered the money along with a pile of fabrics that would become my next dress. I'd make one for a job interview. Irene had already loaded her car. My gaze lifted to the kitchen table where I recalled Ellie sitting for therapy stretches after operations that helped her legs recover from polio at age six. Once we settled secretly in Wisconsin, Ellie and I would have a table where only peaceful dinners would be enjoyed in our new place.

"Shall we go, then?" Irene asked me once I returned to the bedroom.

"One more thing I've got to do."

In my room, I slid my hand under my mattress, feeling around for a note I penned in the bathroom one night and hid away for the right time. My pulse ticked heavily in my fingertips as I placed the note on Joe's pillow.

Iced Out

Joe,

You say you love me, but not the way I deserve to be loved. It took a long time for me to realize this. You refuse to change your ways. You won't seek help at the church. You broke my heart, my bones, and caused me more pain than you'll ever know. It's gone on way too long.

Ellie deserves to be independent. I'm going to give her the opportunities that you've stifled. You set our son Tom free with his own car and a future. Now Ellie will be free to pursue her interests. She is safe with me. Don't try to find us. And don't bother my siblings. They know nothing about my whereabouts.

Carol

The phone rang, but I had no time to answer. I joined Irene on the step and locked the door. Having had to learn to drive in secret, since Joe wouldn't teach me, I prayed for this day for years. Now I had my late father's car, stashed at the cottage, another secret from Joe, at the ready.

The sky turned an eerie pink before the storm, a dark layer of clouds floating in between but still distant. Lady, our family dog, interrupted the quiet. I let her out of the car to roam. The full trunk of the old Ford took three full slams to stay shut, much smaller than Irene's roomy trunk. We had two hours before the storm would hit. If there was ever a time to leave with Ellie and save our lives from Joe's violent abuse, it was now. My brother Wally and his wife, Irene, helped us secure a safe place to go.

Dark gray clouds overtook the pink, and pent-up flurries fell, the snowflakes taking their time to hit the ground as the lacy specks melted. I looked to the heavens. "Mom, if you can hear me, spread your angel wings wide. I need to slow down this storm. I need more time."

"You got everything?" Irene said, locking up the cottage. "You better go get Ellie before they dismiss school. It's already 2:30."

I hugged Irene and promised I'd call her and Wally that evening once we got settled at the rental place.

When I pulled up to the school, buses were already waiting at the doors. I didn't think much of it and parked in the visitor's lot, walking briskly to the office, careful not to slip on the pavement speckled with sticking flakes.

"Didn't you get the call?" the office secretary greeted me. "We called all the numbers on file. We dismissed classes early and are closing before the roads get bad."

"Oh, that's why the buses are already at the door. Is Ellie already on one of them? Which one? I've got to get her off that bus. She can't go directly home."

The secretary started looking at logs for the bus number.

"I should tell you for the record, we're moving. I'll send a note to the principal." As the secretary nodded, I turned as soon as she responded with the bus number, ran down the hall, and flung open the school doors.

Iced Out

The blowing snow stung my face as my breath joined the cloud of exhaust from the buses' diesel engines. "Wait, Wait!" I yelled, waving my arms. I couldn't see through the bus windows, fogged with children's excited breath, happy to be let out of school early. Snow was coming down faster. The bus numbers were whited out with the cold wet snow. I used my sleeve to clear the back window of the car. I tried every switch and finally found the one to turn on wipers. I took on the persona of a pilot in a cockpit preparing for take-off: gas tank has fuel, check the mirrors, (rolled windows down to clear snow), headlights switched on.

A bus parade took off down the street, all equipped with lift gates to accommodate students. I followed the one that turned right, knowing it had several students to drop off first. I planned to intercept it. When it stopped five blocks away, it would take a while to get the hydraulic gate down and up. I parked and left my vehicle. Lady barked like mad as I ran ahead to the open bus door, the driver helping a student down. "Good afternoon sir! I'm Ellie Westchester's mom. Can I take her from here?"

"Who?" he said, holding out his hand to steady a wheelchair onboard.

I climbed aboard at the front and scanned the rows of students. "Ellie?"

"She takes bus No. 40. This is the 42 bus," a boy in a red cap and scarf said.

My wet glove pressed against my forehead in disbelief. I had followed the wrong bus! I ran back to the car to start out again, tracking her bus. As I drove, I contemplated waiting out the storm and leaving after Joe went to work the next day. But would the roads be plowed? What would I do with this car, all loaded? Joe would come home baffled about where I was all day, no food on the table, and I'd be in for a calamity. It was easier to go ahead with the plan. The roads weren't that bad. The wipers offered a clear view of a bus way ahead that was very close to my house. I followed it, no way to get ahead. The next swipe of snow cleared from the window and there it was, pulled over on my block to drop her off. I saw Ellie go down its steps, her back to me, walking slowly, her heel dragging snow while the other left a clear footprint.

I beeped the horn and stuck my head out the window, snow pinching my face. "Hey, Ellie! We have to go. I have all your things."

"We're leaving, now? In Grandpa's car?"

"No time for questions. Hurry." The bus pulled forward, giving her a clear view and more space to walk toward where I parked. She opened the door and saw Lady happily barking to greet her. Ellie unlocked her brace and swung her leg inside, brushing off the snow. The door was closing when we both heard Joe's voice calling from nearby. "Ellie! Is that you? Hey!"

I looked in the side mirror to see Joe walking toward our vehicle. Objects may be closer than they appear. "Don't answer him. Roll up the windows, quick!"

"Shouldn't we say goodbye to Dad?"

"He'll never let us leave, honey. I left a note."

Iced Out

Of all the bad luck, I thought. The school must have called him at work to alert about the storm and early school closing when they couldn't reach me.

I cranked the wheel and pushed the gas pedal measuredly as the old car sputtered and caught traction. Joe was at the curb, stupefied. "He's jogging toward us, Mom."

"Open that glove compartment. There's a pouch in there with a map. I've got to get on the highway. Do we get on Highway 55? Or does it say to go south to bypass downtown? I know you can figure it out. Uncle Wally marked it for us."

"We have to drive north. Yes, take Highway 55."

Living in the city, it was easy to know which way was north. All grid streets, no circle curves to get one confused. I had taken the bus, north-bound and south-bound, to the hospital many times. I recognized the avenues from the bus stops I knew well: Cicero, Pulaski, Kedzie, Western.

"We have to go west to an entrance ramp. There's a sign for the Highway."

Ellie kept her eyes on the map while I glared at red lights. I was in control of the car, of our lives, of our future, but I could not control the timing of red lights. I looked in the rear-view mirror for Joe's car. Traffic was heavy. If he was following us, we had at least a 10-minute head start. I contemplated getting off the highway and taking side roads, but if he was close behind, he would see me exit.

Iowa [W]rites of Winter

I found a familiar road going north. I kept checking the mirror. Traffic thinned, making me feel sure I would have noticed if he was following. We were on Archer Avenue, near where Ellie had to get her special shoes, close to the end of the avenue when it turns to State Street. If I saw him, I'd get as close to the shoe store as possible, and be in a public space where our favorite store manager would recognize me if he confronted us. The snow was coming down harder as we neared Lake Michigan. Not seeing his car behind me, I took a turn to the west to find the highway again.

To keep calm, I asked Ellie to tell me about her day. I had to act like it was a normal thing, she and I, traveling by car, alone. Another first. We always had Joe as a chauffeur. The lakefront effect snow was behind us. "This storm is blowing southeast. Chicago and northern Indiana will see six inches before the front moves through, but northern Illinois and Wisconsin will be clear and dry."

"Mom, you are driving great. I have to go to the restroom soon. Can we stop?"

"Hold it. Please. I don't know if your father is following us."

"Did you tell my school I was leaving?"

"Yes, I stopped in to see the office. I have a letter ready for the principal stating that you'll be transferring, and I picked up your transcripts ahead of time. Your new high school is ready to welcome you. It's small. Public. They don't have stairs, so you will have no barriers. Children of all abilities and ages. The town is amazing. You'll find work, new friends, and we'll both be safe. No more walking on eggshells. We'll eat when we're hungry, sleep when we're tired, go where we want to. Just the two of us."

I explained to Ellie that I sent notes to all the relatives, and she'd see her brother Tom on winter break. "His school is even closer to our new apartment than it is to Chicago.

With the clear skies ahead, we would make it to Lake Geneva before dark. I kept looking behind us for Joe's Chevy. Any light blue car made my heart jump, and snow-covered hoods made every car suspicious. My bladder could not go one mile further. We stopped at a rest stop that had a McDonald's. A crowded place, a mindful choice in case of any confrontation. I used some of my cash to buy our first-ever McDonald's hamburgers and a large pack of fries. "I've got a budget plan for us, Ellie. We can treat ourselves today."

Ellie's face lit up. "This is a treat. I've never had McDonald's."

"Me neither." We purposely sat in the center of the restaurant, away from the windows. We crunched away, pretending we'd be eating French fries from now on, whenever it suited us. I'd rather not feel on edge when enjoying a taste of freedom.

"Ellie, this is going to be the start of many firsts. You will do much more in a small town. Your grandfather left me this car and some money. I can stretch it to get fries again this month once we get settled and we both find work. I'll be sewing, and you can study, even get a job, too. There's only one bank in the town, and Uncle Wally set up an account for us with my inheritance. If anything ever happens to me, you and Tommy are the beneficiaries."

"Why would you say that?"

"I'm just being cautious."

We finished quickly and headed back to the car. I asked her to still be on the lookout for Joe's car. She put my mind at ease with light conversation.

"Can we name this car? I know Dad calls his Chevy 'Blue Bolt.'"

"How about Liberty? This Ford is our wheels to liberty."

"You can call it Liberty, Mom. I'm gonna call it Derby, like a roller derby. Driving 'Derby' is as close to roller skating as I'll ever get."

"Derby, huh? Okay." I looked at Ellie's smiling face. She never complained about not being able to do certain things, like roller skating or skiing. She always kept her upbeat demeanor, concentrating on what she could do. Look at her now, ready to start a new life with me, leaving a horrid predicament. Joe would not let her learn to drive or work. She deserved new horizons, where she could thrive as a young woman of 18.

The horizon met harvested cornfields blanketed by snow. The sun stayed hidden, just like we intended to be.

"I sure will miss Mary."

"We'll get to see your friend again one day.

Iced Out

Think about all the new people you'll meet."

"I do hope people at this public school won't stare at me. After attending a school for the disabled, I'm used to seeing crutches and wheelchairs parked in halls or at desks.I hope they won't find me to be odd."

"I'm optimistic about it. Small towns have had their share of polio cases. With combined grades sharing classrooms in small towns, I bet it won't be unusual to see a student wearing a brace or using crutches. Besides, now that you are older, assimilating with the main population will give you experience. You'll finally be able to get a job nearby, and deal with the public. The public will love interacting with you, Ellie. You will shine."

"I hope so."

Lady was stretched out with her legs over some soft bags holding our towels and bedding. As we turned on a narrower country road, I asked Ellie to be our map reader again as we got closer to town. I was in control, a rare feeling.

As we came to a four-way stop sign on a farm road, the next sign was for Lake Geneva. Population 1200. I chuckled. This would be a big change from urban to rural living. Our former Chicago neighborhood church had about that many members.

We found Main Street, driving slowly to see the shops and restaurants, then turned on East Street to find Darwin. Our rental was the second one from the corner, a white wood house.

"Hey, it's cute!" Ellie popped open the lock

and Lady sensed a change and was ready to pounce out.

I didn't care what it looked like. We had keys to a safe place, and assurances my siblings would not reveal our location to Joe. Our door was beneath an overhung green roof. A For Rent sign was leaning against the wall of the long porch. Stairs from a back door led down a small hill to the woods with lots of land. We were used to chain-linked fences. The four-pane windowed door opened to a carpeted front room, cream wallpaper, a small hallway with a large bedroom on the right and a full bath on the left. The second bedroom was upstairs. "Ellie, you'll get the master bedroom here since it's on the first floor. I'll take the one upstairs."

"Are you sure, Mom? I can climb stairs."

"I know you can, but I'd rather you save your strength for the school days. I don't mind a single, small bedroom at all."

I was bracing for a musty old smell but the whole place smelled of north woods pine, not the Cracker Jack factory. The view from the kitchen window revealed a clump of birch trees and elms, and some tall pines set back. "We need to buy Lady an extra-long leash for this property to prevent her from getting lost in those backwoods."

It was very peaceful, but strange not to see the concrete of our city home alleys framing the block. The two bedrooms were carpeted with a low pile that was no risk for Ellie's brace snagging. The kitchen was adequate. I'd miss counter space, but under a bay window was a small table for an eat-in kitchen space, reminding me of the cottage. The living room was large and cold with a chandelier hanging over nothing, space for a nice dinette set. I could imagine a piano there, since we wouldn't have company. I placed our moving trunk there, to block a path where I'd likely hit my head on the hanging light fixture from the low ceiling. Being tall had its disadvantages.

I was eager to call Wally. "We made it!"

"How's the storm up there? Is there much snow?"

"The roads had a dusting but it was blowing, and then all was dry the farther north we got. There's snow on the ground here that must have fallen weeks ago, but walks are shoveled."

"It really piled up high here. You are lucky you left when you did."

"I have to say, I'm still rattled. The school called Joe and work, and he saw us leave as I was getting Ellie. I drove away as fast as I could. We never even stopped for a toilet break until we crossed the state line. Do you think he'll find us?"

"That car drives well for an old clunker. He won't have any idea about where you were headed, and you would have seen him by now. We didn't ever talk about our place up north when we were at family gatherings. I don't think he even knows I own a place in Geneva."

"Good point. Do you think he'll look at our old house we grew up in? I know it's sold, and maybe occupied already, but Joe doesn't know that. I fear he will break down the door looking for us.”

“Damn, he’d be trespassing if he went over there. I’m not going out tonight, and I’m not sure he would either. Roads are a mess. Play it safe, Carol, and keep your place shut tight, window shades closed. Even if everyone’s staying home tonight, you keep your head down.”

“I will. There are front drapes I can close. I wish there was a garage to hide the car. Anyway, thanks for setting us up here, Wally. It’s lovely. Just what we needed. Give my best to Irene. She was wonderfully helpful. Love you both.”

“Sure. Love you too, Sis.”

We weren’t very hungry and were eager to call it a day. After unpacking necessities, I said goodnight to Ellie. As I settled down upstairs, Lady stayed at the foot of the bed, sniffing and circling her place on the quilt. Usually she’d lie next to the wheezing radiator pipes in our house. My head hit the pillow in utter exhaustion, welcoming the white noise of the central heat whistling through the vents. My headache disappeared, relishing the quiet. I stopped thinking, and let deep sleep come.

***

The six a.m. sunrise spread dimly through the old framed window. I didn’t want curtains to block the natural light. Tree branches swayed, and I felt a cold draft as I passed one of the windows upstairs. A distant wind chime crackled the air pleasantly from a neighbor’s porch. I padded downstairs, careful not to wake Ellie. The front room fireplace was swept clean. I reached inside its dark walls, feeling for a damper lever. Lady wagged and barked as I pulled on my wool coat over my bathrobe. "Shh! Okay, let's go." I could go out freely, without Joe to accuse that I was going out to flirt with a neighbor.

I took the extra step of putting a leash on her as she would roam the snowy land. I didn't miss the pollution noise or hazy odors. The distant Chicago skyline with its Lake Michigan windchill faded to a gentler, yet still cold, flat landscape with shadows of thick bare branches gracing the grounds, a bigger canopy of shadows than back home.

I sleepily walked the perimeter of the house to look for stacks of wood. There was a tarp beneath the steps. Lifting it, Lady sniffed for mice between a short pile of five quartered logs. Perfect to get us through a few nights! Lady pulled me to the birch trees at the end of the property where she could explore. Once she did her business, I tugged her toward the house again. At the back step, I smelled coffee. The light was on in the kitchen. There was Ellie, setting out two cups. Her calm presence and acceptance of the situation was soothing. Lady shook off any snow on her snout and fur. I hung my coat on a panel of hooks nailed above the door stop.

"Good morning! Let's sit in the front room and make a fire. I've got to find matches. How unusual not to have a lighter in the house, huh?"

"We can get some the next time we go to the store." Ellie motioned with her cup to point my gaze to the dining area built-in cabinet. "What a great place for my books."

Iowa [W]rites of Winter

"One day, I'll go back for my mom's place settings and silver. That china cabinet deserves a display, no matter how modest. But yes, there are plenty of shelves for our books."

After we ate oatmeal, Ellie put the two books I had brought for her on the shelves, and I added my prized vase from Sam, my male friend from church. He wrote about Ellie's ordeal with polio in his Chicago Sun Times column. We didn't have much else to unpack. I hated to keep the front room drapes closed but it was smart to be cautious. The lack of light was a sullen reminder of why we moved.

The next day, I found the local grocery store to get some basics: toilet paper, fresh veggies, bouillon cubes, and bread. I grabbed a few free matchbooks at the adjacent liquor store where I pulled out extra cash and bought a pint of brandy to warm my bones. Next, we found the train station, and I stopped.

"What are you doing here, Mom?"

"I'm picking up a schedule. It's good to know our options for the summer."

"Mary could take the train here to visit me."

"Yes, I bet she'll do that to see you."

Cumulus clouds floated by a sapphire sky, not a gray cloud interrupting the horizon. No horns, freight trains, or traffic. The snowy fields beyond the house exposed brown grass with snow drifts blown against hills and barns along the way. Chimneys bellowed the smell of wood fires, smoke vanishing gently before it reached tree tops.

Iced Out

I inhaled every molecule of this new life. Once inside the rental, we made bologna sandwiches with mustard and pickles.

When the phone rang, I knocked the pickle jar cover to the floor. It clanged and spun on the floor. "Determined, I guess." I hid my worry that it could be Joe. No one had this number except my brother and Irene.

Reluctantly, I picked up the phone. It was Tom. "Son, how did you get this number? Are you ok?"

"Yes, but Dad's not. He got in a wreck. I got your letter that you left him, but the police tracked me down at college to notify me. I called Uncle Wally to get this number."

"The police?"

"Yes, an officer came to my dorm. In person! I'm the only Westchester they could track down. They couldn't reach you. Dad's at St. Mary's Hospital. He crashed during the snowstorm, right into a street pole by Grandma and Grandpa's house. Why would he go there?"

I knew why. He was chasing us, thinking we were headed there. But we headed north to Wisconsin.

"Did you talk to an officer in person?"

"Yeah, I told you that already. I'm still on campus. Mom, should I come home? Where are you?"

"I'm… I'm… I can't say where I am staying

right now, Tom. I wrote to you about why."

"Dad always says mean stuff, but now he's banged up. He can't hurt you now, Mom."

"What exactly did the officer tell you?" I heard Tom inhale a puff, then exhale. He'd taken up smoking at college.

"He asked a lot of questions. I told the cop that you sent me a letter without a forwarding address. I don't want you to be in any trouble, Mom. Sorry if I wasn't supposed to report that. He did ask me if Dad owns a gun. The police confiscated a rifle and said it's at the station in our local precinct."

"Let it be where it is." I shuddered. "Jesus, he was going after us, armed!"

"Mom, please tell me, where are you? Should I pick you up? Or should I meet you at the hospital?"

"No. No. You have classes. I'll figure something out."

I hung up and called the hospital. They confirmed Joe was a patient in critical condition.

I fell silent. The person let me absorb this. "Is he conscious?"

On autopilot, my wifely duty tugged at my conscience. Poor Joe! Crushed by all that metal on impact. Then my mind whirled back to reality. He brought his loaded gun in the car. I crushed up the grocery bag and threw it on the floor.

Iced Out

Ellie clanked the pickle jar cap back on the table. "Earth to Mom! Please tell me what happened!"

"Your father is…he's… in the hospital. He wrecked the car."

"I knew we should have said goodbye." Ellie's eyes teared up. "I don't want Dad to die."

"I know you don't. But I have to tell you something. He had a gun in the car. Tommy said so. And there is something else."

"A gun?"

I nodded my head yes. "It also could have been the car's brakes. Your Dad threatened me to not take the car cause he would tamper with it. Or it could simply have been the storm, him driving too fast, God knows. We have to face it, Ellie. Your dad is responsible for where he is right now."

I asked my sister Polly to go to the hospital. After hours of talking, we figured out a way for me to talk to Joe on the phone, if he was conscious. Once she made it there, she called me from his hospital room. I heard the rhythm of swooshes in the background. She told me when she'd be putting the phone to his ear. My throat felt tight when I tried to speak.

"Joe. It's me." I paused to see if he'd say anything back. "I'm sorry you're hurt. I hope the drugs are working and you're not feeling the horrid pain like you have caused me repeatedly. No one deserves the anguish you put me through." There was no response. I spoke louder in case he couldn't hear me in his foggy state.

"Know that your children are the only ones that might come to your side—and that I will not. Ever. Again. Our marriage is dead to me. I know you had your gun and you want me dead for leaving you. Or were you going to be a coward, ready to threaten me if I didn't return? Or hit me again, knowing I can't defend myself against you? I'll keep your gun now, when I get it back from the police. I'll be filing a restraining order." I ran out of gumption, going beyond what I had planned to say. Silence.

Then I heard a commotion of rapid beeps. A nurse's voice was next: "Clear the room!" Click. The line went dead.

My thoughts ricocheted from worry to anger to guilt. I had to get a hold of Polly, not only to find out what was happening but also to ask about how to get a restraining order. Now I really needed one.

Polly rang a few minutes later. "Are you sitting down?"

"No, but I'm here. What is going on there? Is he awake? Does he want to talk?"

"It's over, Sis. He's—he's—gone. They worked on him, but nothing." She paused. "What did you say to him?"

My spine tingled. Everything became still except for a sudden crackling in the fireplace, glowing as if an angel sparked it to warm me in glorious comfort, a release from his grasp, forever. "Tell me again, Polly."

"Joe's met his maker, Carol."

Iced Out

Ellie and I were finally free.

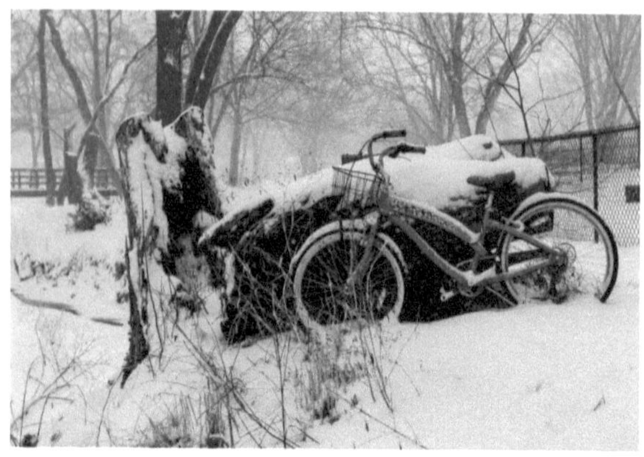

Abandoned

William Ford

To Drive Up a Hill

Rachel Schneberger

47

The tires refused to grip,
no longer a snowy façade,
I found ice,
the blackest kind,
a glaze,
it's smooth surface
removes control.
I can't accelerate,
neither brake,
if I'm lucky,
I'll just float
back
down

Escape From Iowa Winter: A Text Adventure

G.Z. Chapman

LAST NIGHT A FOOT OF SNOW FELL AND HARDENED INTO CEMENT ON TOP OF THE EXISTING SNOW. TO ESCAPE, JUST DRIVE AWAY IN YOUR CAR.

YOU HAVE SELECTED ADVANCED MODE (IOWA).

GO CAR

THERE IS NO CAR.

WALK SOUTH

YOU CANNOT! THERE IS SNOW IN THE WAY.

CLEAR SNOW

WITH WHAT?

USE SHOVEL

YOU DO NOT HAVE: THE SHOVEL

GET SHOVEL

shovel (1 point)

CLEAR SNOW WITH SHOVEL

Escape From Iowa Winter

snow cleared 2 hours (1 point)

GO CAR

THERE IS NO CAR.

WALK SOUTH

YOU WALK SOUTH.

GO CAR

YOU CANNOT REACH: THE CAR.

CLEAR SNOW WITH SHOVEL

YOU MUST CLEAR SNOW OFF CAR FIRST.

CLEAR SNOW OFF CAR

YOU DO NOT HAVE: THE BRUSH. YOU DO
NOT HAVE: THE SCRAPER.

GET BRUSH

brush1 IS MISSING (YOU ARE IN ADVANCE
MODE)

brush2 IS BURIED UNDER LUMBER,
BEHIND A SEAT, IN A LOCKED TRUCK
(YOU ARE IN ADVANCE MODE)

brush3

GET BRUSH3

I DO NOT UNDERSTAND.

GET brush3

I DO NOT UNDERSTAND.

DELETE brush1

brush1 DELETED

DELETE brush2

brush2 DELETED

GET BRUSH

YOU DO NOT HAVE: THE BRUSH

GO CAR

YOU CANNOT REACH: THE CAR

CLEAR SNOW WITH SHOVEL

YOU MUST CLEAN SNOW OFF CAR FIRST.

CLEAR SNOW OFF CAR

YOU DO NOT HAVE: THE BRUSH

YOU DO NOT HAVE: THE SCRAPER

BRUSH SNOW

THE CEMENT SNOW IS TOO HARD. TRY
THE SCRAPER?

SCRAPE SNOW

Escape From Iowa Winter

YOU DO NOT HAVE: THE SCRAPER

WHERE SCRAPER?

THE SCRAPER IS IN THE CAR.

WHERE BRUSH?

THE BRUSH IS IN THE CAR.

BRUSH SNOW BY HAND

THE CEMENT SNOW IS TOO HARD. TRY THE SCRAPER?

USE DYNAMITE

YOU DO NOT HAVE: DYNAMITE

CHISEL

YOU DO NOT HAVE: THE SCRAPER

GET IN CAR

YOU CANNOT REACH: THE CAR

I WILL DELETE YOU

OKAY, BUT IT WILL COST YOU ONE LIFE.

YOU HAVE DIED. THAT WILL COST YOU ONE LIFE.

SCORE

You have earned 2 points out of 1,000.

You have used 2.5 hours.

You have used 1 lives. Better hurry.

YOU HAVE FOUND THE CAR. SORT OF.

GET SCRAPER

THE SCRAPER IS OUT OF REACH.

GET BRUSH

THE BRUSH IS OUT OF REACH.

EXIT CAR

OK

WALK AROUND CAR

OKAY, BUT THE ICE BOULDERS ARE 3 FEET HIGH, IT IS VERY SLICK, AND YOU ARE LIKELY TO BE EATEN BY A GRUE.

FUNNY

I once patched a running RTS system and it stayed up for almost 3 seconds.

FUNNY

I once patched a running RTS system and it stayed up for almost 3 seconds.

FUNNY

I once patched a running RTS system and it stayed up for almost 3 seconds.

Escape From Iowa Winter

OPEN PASSENGER DOOR

THE PASSENGER DOOR IS CEMENTED
SHUT.

GET BRUSH

YOU DO NOT HAVE: THE BRUSH

GET SCRAPER

YOU DO NOT HAVE: THE SCRAPER

WALK AROUND CAR

OKAY, BUT THE ICE BOULDERS ARE 3
FEET HIGH, IT IS VERY SLICK, AND YOU
ARE LIKELY TO BE EATEN BY A GRUE.

ALERT! YOU HAVE BEEN EATEN BY A
GRUE. IT DIDN'T MUCH ENJOY IT
EITHER. SHALL I USE SOME ORANGE
SMOKE AND FIX YOU UP? (YES)

YES

ENTER CAR

OPEN PASSENGER WINDOW

PASSENGER WINDOW IS ICED SHUT
OUTSIDE THE CAR--USE THE SCRAPER?

GET SCRAPER

THE SCRAPER IS OUT OF REACH.

I WILL DELETE YOU AND YOUR

INSTALLATION CD

DID YOU MEAN HINT?

HINT PASSENGER

UPON ENTERING CAR INSERT KEY (STARTING INVENTORY) WARM CAR, WARM INTERIOR, WARM REAR WINDOW WIRE DEFROSTERS.

SCORE

You have earned 2 points out of 1,000.

You have used 3 hours.

You have used 2 lives. Better hurry.

INSERT KEY

OK

START CAR

OK

TURN ON DEFROSTERS

OK

TURN ON REAR WINDOW WIRE DEFROSTERS

OK

IS CAR WARM?

Escape From Iowa Winter

NO

WAIT UNTIL CAR IS WARM

OK

ALERT! CAR IS NOW WARM (1 point)

SCORE

You have earned 3 points out of 1,000.

You have used 3.5 hours.

You have used 2 lives. Better hurry.

I HATE YOU

I DO NOT UNDERSTAND YOUR REQUEST.

EXIT CAR

OK

WALK AROUND CAR

OKAY, BUT THE ICE BOULDERS ARE 3 FEET HIGH, IT IS VERY SLICK, AND YOU ARE LIKELY TO BE EATEN BY A GRUE.

OPEN PASSENGER

THAT SIDE IS FROZEN SHUT--HAVE YOU TRIED THE DRAGON'S BREATH?

HINT DRAGON'S BREATH

I DO NOT UNDERSTAND: DRAGON'S

WHERE DRAGON'S-BREATH

YOU HAVE TO DRIVE YOUR CAR EAST OF THE SUN.

DRIVE CAR

THE CAR IS EMBEDDED IN 32 INCHES OF SNOW PLOW CEMENT.

HINT CAR

YOU NEED THE WRIT OF PHARAMOND TO ARRIVE ALIVE IN THIS WEATHER.

WHERE WRIT OF PHARAMOND?

I DO NOT UNDERSTAND.

WHERE WRIT-PHARAMOND?

YOU NEED TO DRIVE YOUR CAR TO THE JUXTAPOSITION OF TWO MAJOR ROADS.

HOW CAN I DRIVE MY BLEEPING BLEEPING CAR IT IS STUCK IN AN ICE AGE MASTODON SIZED BLOCK OF ICE/ SNOW CEMENT YOU BLEEPING STUPID MORONIC GAME!

DO YOU WISH TO QUIT?

NO

USE SHOVEL

YOU HAVE NO SHOVEL.

WHERE SHOVEL?

A THIEF TOOK: THE SHOVEL INTO A MAZE OF TWISTY LITTLE PASSAGES, ALL ALIKE.

IN THIS WEATHER?

I DO NOT UNDERSTAND.

I WILL DELETE YOU AND YOUR INSTALLATION CD AND EVERY VERSION OF YOU ON EVERY COMPUTER EVERYWHERE

DUDE, YOUR MOM SCARES ME MORE THAN YOU DO.

WHERE MOM?

YOUR MOM TOOK THE SHOVEL YOU WERE USING TO DIG OUT INSTEAD OF GETTING ONE OF HER OWN--SHE IS OVER AT THE NEIGHBORS CLEANING OFF THEIR DRIVEWAY.

Aaaaaaarrrrrrrrrrrrrrrrrrrrrrgggggghhh!

I DO NOT UNDERSTAND.

USE DRAGON'S-BREATH

YOU DO NOT HAVE: THE DRAGON'S-BREATH

"I don't have the Dragon's Breath? We'll see about that"

POKE C927,0003

POKE E8F2,03A1

CHECK INVENTORY

OH! YOU DO HAVE THE DRAGON'S BREATH HOW DID YOU DO THAT?

exception catch 9102 mainc

exception catch 9102 mainc

exception catch 9102 mainc

USE DRAGON'S BREATH

YOU DO NOT HAVE: 'DRAGON'

USE DRAGON'S-BREATH

OK

THE ICE MELTS.

THE EXTENDABLE BRUSH MELTS.

THE SCRAPER MELTS.

THE PASSENGER DOOR MELTS.

THE CAR MELTS.

YOU MELT.

OH DEAR, THAT WAS YOUR LAST LIFE.

THE CAR SPRINGS TO LIFE AS THE ICE MELTS.

Escape From Iowa Winter

segmentation fault 302

Polar Vortex

Dennis Maulsby

Boots kick up rhinestone snow grit.
Expelled breath freezes. Hard rime frost

stiffens the fur of my parka hood.
Arctic needles tattoo nose, cheeks.

I hawk and spit.
Frozen phlegm rattles over white crust.

A dervish whirlwind churns ice spangles
up sleeves and pant legs.

Knots of flakes cloud my glasses.
Blue-crystal fangs gnaw fingers, toes.

An ice-braided demon wind-shrieks,
"I'll kill you if I can!"

In the Bleak Midwinter

Malcolm MacDougall

From the last diaries of Giordiano Lingotti, an itinerant painter whose death in the upper reaches of what would become Northern Italy went unnoticed until his diaries were discovered in 2003:

November 3rd, 1593, Evening

This morning, I was painting Lord Sforza in a pose with his leg braced against the chest at the base of his bed. He gripped his old sword tight, leaning nearly his full weight on it to avoid the agony of his gouty foot. He wore black velvet in a style that reminded me of the Borgia boy, gloomy and dark, though the boy wore it to impress and terrify whereas I felt Lord Sforza simply owned nothing better.

He demanded I paint him with jewels, though he wore none. I asked him what sort of jewels he preferred. It was better not to inquire why. In this area, lords come in one streak—temperamental, quick to violence, and deeply insecure about their family origins. North of Florence is nothing but a hundred tiny nation-states with former mercenaries running them as if they still commanded armies instead of peasants.

He was a bulky man, the quintessential former soldier run to fat, but he still carried himself with an aura of coiled danger. He told me that I should paint him with the sort of gems worn by the other lords.

Iowa [W]rites of Winter

I cast my mind through my previous clients. I remembered the bare necks I adorned with thick gold chains, the pendulous breasts of wives hanging low that I'd pulled up and glossed over, the tin circlets I'd burnished into golden diadems.

I chose a simple ring and a pendant I remembered from my days in Florence—tasteful, subtle, and of course a fiction. Such is the life of a traveling painter. We are but editors to reality.

The room that they have given me is chilly. The windowsill is rimed with frost and the shutters are sealed loosely. I have assembled somewhat of a nest out of the rank furs of rabbit and fox I took on my trip.

The lord's wife is gone this night on a hunting trip. I hear the faint trump of horns echoing over the hills from the woods, though it is near impossible to tell the direction from whence they come. She has gone with the game warden, her handmaiden, and one donkey bearing the equipment.

November 4th, 1593, Morning

There has been an accident. The lady came back late last night after I had fallen into a fitful sleep. Her horse startled on the path, spooked by a snake that somehow survived until this November chill. The priest says it bodes of Satan's influence. It may be the case. I am given to understand that the lady is an accomplished horsewoman, but she was hurled from her horse head-first onto a stone.

In the Bleak Midwinter

The weather turned when I awoke this morning, sending drifts of snow in through the cracks of the shutters. The bottom of my makeshift bed was soaked by the melting snow and it was near-intolerable to emerge from my bedclothes into the cold. I peered outside as I shuffled on my heaviest coat and tunic. The road was unrecognizable. I had hoped that I would be only three days here, but it seems I must stay for the foreseeable future.

I was told of the lady's fall by the kitchen servants. There are two of them—gossipy, lithe little youths, one male, one female—who so closely resemble each other it is difficult to believe that they are not siblings. They assure me they are not related, merely close, and with the way they spill over each other like newborn kittens I pray it to be true. They are paler than the snow outside. They tell me they are from the far north, from the Swedish isles. I do not know of any isles of the Swedes but they assure me that they originate from there, that they were servants to a great warlord whose travels ranged as far as Egypt before they came here.

They asked me if I had heard the commotion early that morning and I told them truthfully that I had not. My room sits on the opposite side of the fortress. They said, tittering with unseemly glee, that the lord Sforza had roared "like a bull getting castrated". I had heard nothing.

I devoured the meal they had prepared me and excused myself. I feel increasingly discomfited by their canny stares and their strange whispers. They speak a language among each other I do not understand.

Iowa [W]rites of Winter

I appeared in the Lord's chambers, prepared for another day of painting. He was absent, and so I wandered the rooms of the fortress. The fortress is a remarkable, ancient thing, made of the black granite that makes up the mountain range around us. It sits as a square, four walls surrounding a central court, with a single bridge spanning the gap from the main road. The rest of the fortress stands at the edge of a great precipice, its feet set at the edge like a man on the verge of hurling himself in. I can barely stand to walk along the parapets for the sickness of the drop next to me. I roamed the great central hall, which at some point in a wealthier past had been divided into smaller rooms. Nearly all the doors are locked. I saw nobody save the old priest, a Roman whose accent was thick and hampered by a remarkable stutter. He told me (after a great deal of waiting on my part) that the Lord had gone with the Lady to the nearby village to search for someone knowledgeable in medicine. They will return this evening, he says. For now I will peruse the library and its surprisingly extensive selection.

November 4th, 1593, Evening

The lady has returned and I have sighted her for the first time. She is a beautiful woman, comely and fit. They say that she bore two children to Lord Sforza but lost them to the plague that swept the area three years past. Only a minor knot of scars on the left side of her swan-like neck betray the deathly illness she suffered as she cared for the two. The servants in the kitchen tell me that she refused to allow anyone else be exposed to the miasma of their room. She commanded them to ring the outside of the door with flowers and incense to ward off the sickly scent of the dying children.

She is brilliant as well—the library's volume is due to her influence. She came to the fortress a decade ago as a girl of sixteen and brought the ancient priest with her. Now she looks weak, faint. She wears a simple dress with no adornment as if there are no guests at all in her abode. I know I am of no real repute, but I feel as if I have been forgotten about entirely. I shall leave once the painting is complete.

They could not find the witching-woman – the priest says that she may have died in the cold. He obviously bears a hatred for the superstitions of the villagers so he cannot be trusted to be objective.

She complains of a headache that feels like a fire in her skull. It prickles, she says, sends rippling waves of pain through her. Indeed, she seems to waver and sway like seaweed in a tide, never upright, constantly on the verge of falling until finally escorted to her bed by her handmaiden. She is in good hands, I feel. The handmaiden is a sour-faced woman of some twenty-five years, stout and thick. She commands like a lord in battle, with an intensity that brooks no objection and stirs the body to action against the will of its owner.

The snow has continued to fall throughout the day and the windows glow with the strange half-light of the winter gloaming. I write this last in the guttering light of a tallow-candle but must retire.

Iowa [W]rites of Winter

November 5th, 1593, Afternoon

I ate again with the tittering ghosts that haunt the kitchen. They have told me their names. The boy is Huginn and the girl is Muninn. They have grown stranger, I think, the more I have seen of them. Their eyes have the glittering look of goats' eyes, too wide, the iris too big and too moist. They run their hands through each others' hair, trace the earlobe of the other with a delicate pale finger or tap their foreheads gently together, looking into each others' bizarre eyes. I wonder what the old priest thinks of them, if the old thing can think at all.

The lady retreated to her library. She wears a carefully applied yet inexpert bandage wrapped around her head in such a way that it hangs low over her eyes. She gazed at her books of medicine—Galen, Paracelsus, and other, newer texts from battle-time doctors—through a veil of bloody gauze. I did not expect her when I wandered in, still not able to locate Lord Sforza. After a brief spate of apologies and confusion she welcomed me and bade me sit. She pointed out a book she had a particular fondness for and recommended, a brief tome on the natural fauna of the region.

We were silent for a short time until it felt so quiet one could hear the worms boring their way through the books. It was then that she turned towards me, eyes wide underneath the gauze, and spat out a proposition so vile I hesitate to even think of it. She spoke as if the words were hot coals on her tongue.

Immediately she burst into tears of shame so excessive they startled me nearly as much as the vile proposition. The book she held fell to the floor as she fled. I picked it up and glanced through the pages, but my Latin was too poor to comprehend much. I could only understand a striking illustration of the head of a man with an expression of great agony. The point of a drill bore into his temple. A trickle of bright red blood traced its way down the side of his open, screaming mouth. It disturbed me greatly and I hurriedly closed the book.

I have been summoned at last to continue the portrait. I fear that it may be affected by the injury, that the Lord may be too unsettled to make a good pose. I will have to improvise more than ever to redeem the image to my own standards, let alone the Lord's.

November 5th, 1593, Evening

The painting session was subdued but Lord Sforza seemed to not be in ill humor. I could not help but wonder if the outburst in the library had been some flight of fancy, a recollection of some coarse fisherman's crass remark. I had often found myself in the criminal areas of Florence before I was exiled, and I could clearly recall the sounds of the muffled curses and deep oaths murmured in the darkness. Perhaps, I thought, I had been confused and misheard something she had said and filled in an old memory.

I suspect I would have erased it from my mind save for supper. Lord Sforza, relieved that the lady seemed to be recovering, had ordered the slaughtered hart cooked over the roasting fire. Though they had not the time nor the stockpile of dried spice to roast the entire beast we were each served a glistening haunch. The food glistened with a weak wine reduction steeped with juniper berries and thyme. It was poor fare in comparison to a Venetian trattatoria, but it tasted like liquid gold on my travel-deadened tongue.

The lady was silent, taking bites so small they barely stayed on the point of her knife. As if to compensate, Lord Sforza roared and laughed as he told some meandering story at the doddering priest and the blank-faced handmaiden. I nodded politely and gnawed at the vegetables—withering turnips and cavolo nero gone to bitterness.

The lady dropped her knife to the floor with a clatter and Lord Sforza turned to her with the attentive focus of a hunting-bird. She stared fixedly at some space beyond the priest's bowed head, into the darkness of the corners of the room where the guttering torches did not reach. She reeled back in her seat, seized as if with some great, terrible fear, shaking like a chilled animal, her mouth hanging open, releasing a guttural, choking noise. Her shaking pulled the bandage loose from her forehead and it slipped down to lie around her neck like a noxious, blood-soaked necklace. The wound looked like an eye in the center of her forehead. It was a perfectly centered horizontal slit, pale bone peeping through the encrusting scabrousness around the edges of the wound.

She raised a trembling hand and pointed into the darkness, her mouth working, forming words that never came. A long moan escaped her.

We looked and saw nothing save the moving shadows of the priest cast by the torches. She broke free of the enchantment and fled, running so quickly her chair was knocked to the floor. She was still emitting that awful animal moan as she ran, that sound like air escaping a finally-dead corpse.

The supper was over then. The Lord Sforza swept away from the table, leaving me, the handmaiden, and the priest to slump over our cold hunks of meat. The twins cleared the plates away and I came back to my room to calculate how long it will be before the painting is finished. The snow continues to fall through the window. I have had to drag my bed to the other side of the room. I swear that I can hear the giggling of the twins echoing down the hall. Why do they roam the halls freely when it seems that the rest of this accursed fortress is trapped in the same miniscule circuits? The priest bumbles back and forth between the chapel and the dining room, the game warden lurking outside with his horses and hawks, the Lord in his room.

I must go to bed. I have started to see movement in the shadows, demoniac figures in the corners of my eyes that turn into cracks in the stone, or flickering shadows cast by my guttering candle, or the ordinary things of a crumbling fortress. I shall sleep. I hope that in the morning this noxious dread will pass, the snow will cease falling, and I can escape this place.

November 6th, 1593, Afternoon

I was awoken by the sound of the Lady's screams, and this time it was loud enough to reach across the whole of the fortress. She was wailing something too distant for me to hear, but I leaped into my clothing and dashed down the halls to see what it was.

When I arrived in the great central hall of the fortress, I came upon a tableau of chaos. The great table in the center of the room was tipped on its side, a crack running down the great plane of its center. The twins and the game warden hovered in the doorway, bobbing back and forth like corks on a troubled pond's surface. The priest had a crucifix in his hand, the other raised towards the Lady. Lord Sforza held her in his arms, crushing her in his thick, hammish arms. She looked tiny, like a toy being shaken by a child.

"You sons of bitches," she spat, "you damned men, I'm not possessed." Her voice dripped with acid hatred as she struggled against her husband's arms. The stuttering priest was murmuring something in Latin, one of the exorcisms the Romans so love to indulge in. "I need a trepanation."

"It'll be alright, my love," the Lord Sforza said, grasping her tighter. His scarred face had the pathetic look of a child who's been struck, confused and uncomprehendingly dull. "The snake has possessed you. You'll be safe soon, I promise."

"My brain is bleeding," she spat. "I need a doctor."

The priest drew closer, waving the crucifix with such vigorous intensity I was afraid he would hit her. She struggled harder, screamed in rage, and then went slack in her husband's arms. For a pensive moment, I wondered if she had simply died. The space of a breath, then another passed before she regained consciousness, her head rolling on her neck, and she smiled at the priest with a perverse look that made my skin crawl.

When she spoke again her voice sounded as if it were boiled in honey. "I see my mother, Benuveto."

The priest recoiled, murmuring sancta marias under his breath. The Lady kept speaking in a rushed voice, still sweet, still trapping the ear. "My mother is rotting, Benuveto. My mother has been dead since we left Urbino. My father killed her and I saw him kill her, Benuveto."

"Speak not, demon," snarled the Lord Sforza. "You are the son of the Prince of Lies."

"Benuveto," said the Lady or the demon, I knew not which, "Why did my father kill her? She points to you."

The priest seemed to gather himself, strode forwards and slapped her across the face with a force that seemed impossible with such frail limbs. The Lord recoiled, shocked, then glared around the room at the lot of us.

"Leave us," he screamed. "Leave us or I swear on the Virgin, I will hang you all from the ramparts."

November 6th, 1593, Evening

The Lord Sforza summoned me to continue the painting. It is nearly complete now. I only need to do the fine detailing work which shall not necessitate his presence, which relieves me as he grows increasingly erratic, full of blustering rage and quiet contemplation in equal measure. His wife is nowhere to be seen, but he tells me that she is resting. I will wait for the latest layer of the paint to dry until the morning, and then I am free to leave, though the snow piles ever higher. The game warden struck out for the village to hunt once again for the witching-woman and has not returned. When he left, the snow was piled near to the tops of his horse's hocks.

That leaves me, the priest, the handmaiden, who has now retreated to Lady Sforza's bedchamber to mind her at all times, and the two ghosts. They seem bolder the more the Lord retreats from the outside of his chambers, eluding their duties and letting the chickens run wild outside of their pens, laughing to see them sinking into the snowdrifts. Were they my servants I would thrash them but it seems Lord Sforza gives them indulgence upon indulgence. Perhaps he fears them.

I have set my easel at the farthest corner of the room and tomorrow will paint throughout the day in an effort to finish before nightfall. I wish to be rid of this place—the carvings in the walls seem to shift and move even in the brightness of day, and I hear the Lady's screams even now, echoing inside of me.

November 7th, 1593, Noon

The Lady joined us in the kitchen for our morning breakfast. She was accompanied by the

In the Bleak Midwinter

two youths, one to each side, holding her hands to support her. They flitted around her like flies in a horse's eyes on a hot summer day, plucking at her hair and adjusting her dress with pinches and pulls straying too close to the flesh underneath.

She no longer wears the bandage. Though the wound no longer bleeds it is still exposed to the air. The white of her delicate skull glows as if it has been polished. She shows it with an air of strange seduction, and it feels more and more as if the demon or sickness that has taken her is gazing out of it into me.

She fixed me with her eerie gaze, and I saw that the blacks of her eyes had expanded so that there was no longer any color, just two pits opening into her head. I did not like to meet that gaze and I chose to invest my attention into my porridge. I had to cook it myself over the guttering coals in the fireplace in the absence of the twins. The handmaiden is nowhere to be seen.

She asked me what other fine lords and ladies I had done portraits for. I told her a few that she might have heard of and made up some others that would be impossible to verify the existence of. She seemed fascinated and kept asking me questions while the two youths leaned against her, and Huginn let down her hair from its tight coils, gazing at me out of the side of his eyes as if daring me to reprimand him. She failed to notice, leaned forward with her chin on her hands, enraptured by my pitiful stories of traveling from Florence to these northern kingdoms.

I made my excuses as I finished my repast and started to scuttle away from the strange threesome, a Cerberus watching my movements with the hunger of a predator. Muninn whispered in her ear breathily, laughing deep in her throat, and the Lady laughed with her before a fit overtook her. I wanted to leave but was frozen watching her as her eyes rolled back in her head and she trembled like a dead leaf in the wind. She foamed at the corners of her mouth, falling back into Huginn and Muninn's arms. A low shriek came from her, a bubbling growl, and she seemed insensitive to the world.

The fit passed as quickly as it came, and she blinked slowly, glancing back and forth between the faces of the two from beneath hooded eyes. She reached up to caress their faces with her long, delicate fingers, tracing their thin lips, their hollow cheeks. They seemed as unperturbed as they had been by her fit, almost gleeful at her touch, thrilling like hounds under the stroke of their master's hand. Her head still in their laps, she looked over at me and beckoned me to them.

She told me she knew why I had been banished from Florence, the crimes done in the sweating dark that I had committed with Buonnarotti. She told me she wanted to know me, that the four of us could be one, and Huginn and Muninn hung over her with matching smiles. I turned and ran, and now I hide here in my room. I have not been summoned yet by the Lord, and so I strive to finish the painting and scribble out these small essays in between layers. I hardly wait for the paint to dry. This accursed snow still falls, but I will venture out even if it comes to above my head. I cannot go without my payment. I must survive here just another day.

The eye in the center of her forehead can see sins. It is a gift from Satan himself. It sees into the

In the Bleak Midwinter

soul, and it plucks out the shames and the sins. It knows what I have done and what we all have done. It sees me still. The shadows move and twist in the gloom, but I dare not open the shutters in fear of the snow burying everything in the room.

November 7th, 1593, Night

The painting is complete but the lord has told me that payment will only be in the morning and so I am trapped here. I have gnawed on the remnants of some dried smoked meat I kept in my satchel for the trip ahead rather than braving Huginn and Muninn. I hid in the hallways, leaping from doorway to doorway in an effort to hide myself from their laughing gaze, their elfin hunt.

I opened the shutters after the snow had ceased falling—blessed, blessed weather, that it would turn so! And I looked out across the courtyard to see whether the path had yet melted or if the game warden had returned, but I saw nothing.

A short while later

I saw across the courtyard to the ramparts on the other side, and I saw him venturing out, that doddering old man, with his back hunched against the cold, staggering out of the tower door. He looked behind him fearfully but did not stop as he ventured out further, followed by Lady Sforza. Her clothes by now are tattered as if she has torn at them with a knife. Though the wind blew chill as it has been since I arrived she did not reel away.

Iowa [W]rites of Winter

They walked on the rampart side by side, she to the inside, until they reached the center of the ramparts where the fortress overlooks the cliff's face. She spoke to him, in words impossible to discern at so great a distance, and he jerked back as she stabbed him in the heart. Then with a strength as great as a lion she seized him by the collar of his cassock and twisted to hurl him over the sides of the ramparts. He fell silent without a scream until he hit the stones below.

She looked at me, I swear it. Across the distance of the courtyard, crouched down as I was with the barest vestige of my eye peering out, still shocked at what I had witnessed, she saw me. And that accursed eye, that thing that sprouted from her milk-white flesh, saw my soul and laughed at me. I am in the deepest fear. I have gathered my things and will demand payment from the lord at once, as the painting is complete.

November 14th, 1593

May I be forgiven. May God forgive me for what I have done, for what I have seen.

I cowered in the room for some time after what I witnessed but after I wrote the last entry I was stirred to a new determination to flee that place. I went to confront the Lord Sforza with my bags packed and the painting in tow to demand my payment but was stopped before I could reach his chambers.

Out in the great chamber, the hulking table still spilled on its side, Lord Sforza stood over the dead bodies of Huginn and Munnin, a long, slender stiletto in his hand. It was a vendetta knife, the tripartite stake that makes wounds impossible to stitch closed. The two youths were naked, sprawled over each other, even in death still smirking, still tangled in each other, their fast-glazing eyes unseeingly staring at the Lord Sforza. He was maddened now, as enraged as a bull freed from its pen, and he turned to me and extended his dagger. I realized Lady Sforza was on the other side of the room slumped unconscious against the wall.

"You," bellowed Lord Sforza. "You brought this demon. You were the one who caused this."

"My Lord," I protested, "I don't know what you mean. Please, allow me to take a pittance of my payment and I'll be gone from your doorstep forever. I cannot leave without my money, Lord. I will starve."

"Then worry not," he barked. "You will not last long enough to feel the pang of your next meal." He surged at me in attack, and in desperation I put the painting between him and I, perhaps in the vain hope that he would be halted by the image of his own visage Instead he careened into me, and the knife bounced off of the wood of the painting as we crashed to the ground. He stared at me over the top of the painting with his cow-like expression of hurt, of confusion. He slid to the ground, dead, his own dagger buried in his stomach. The wood portrait cracked in half underneath his weight.

I backed away, panting, terrified, praying that I would be forgiven this sin. The Lady stirred and I seized the dagger, holding it before me like a talisman. She abandoned the curtain and strode towards me.

She kneeled before me on the cold flagstones and gazed up at me, I still frozen, and with great focus, wrapped her hands one at a time around mine on the blade of the dagger. Thick blood oozed from between her white-knuckled fingers. Her eyes were blue once again, warm and lucid, and she had the look of one who has surfaced from a dive deep into the ocean. She placed the point of the knife in the middle of the wound in her forehead.

"You're trembling," she said, gentle, loving. "It's all right." She pulled at the blade of the knife and it bit into the smooth whiteness of the eye-shaped wound. She glanced to the side. "Flee once you do this thing. Leave me to my sins."

The knife, spurred on by my thrust or her grip, plunged into her forehead. It sank through the front of her skull until it broke through the hard surface to release a gout of blood so intense it stained the front of my breeches and tunic down to my knees and up to my ribs. She fell back at once as the blood spurted from her, and as I fled those halls I could hear her guttural sigh in relief in the middle of that great devastation.

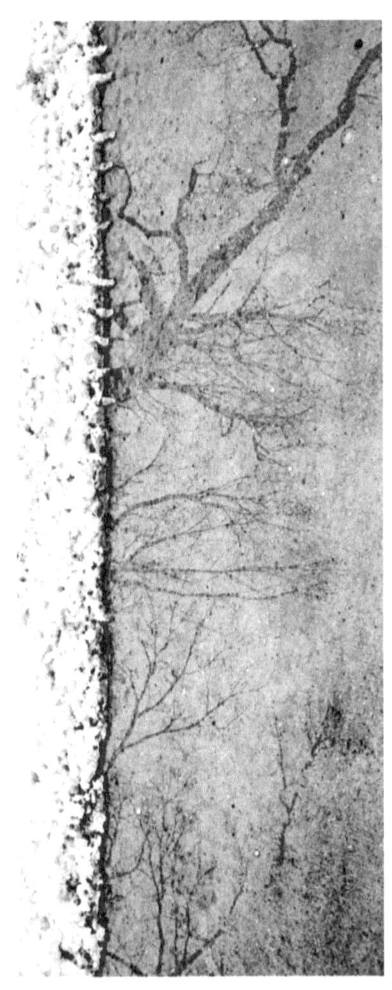

Melted

Kristel Saxon

WINTERBOURNE

Theodore Michelet Sterling

ONE: Jill

A chilly wind snaked through Mother Sarah's coat, a stinging reminder to wear a scarf before leaving the house. Any other solstice she would have hauled her cart home, retrieving her woolen scarf (itchy as it was). Slipping in and out of her cottage would hardly delay her two-day sojourn an hour, but it would buy him time to find her.

Bill Winterbourne's wife wasn't due for another month, but the Winterbournes always…. Mother Sarah had prepared, arranging a midwife, but Bill would somehow drag her into it. The Winterbournes always did.

She bundled up tighter and snapped the reins, urging her mule to pick up the pace.

Dirt-muffled footsteps approached from behind.

Too soon!

Another snap. "C'mon, Muley!"

The footsteps overtook them.

Bill strode beside her, panting. "Your mule's named Muley?"

"Easy to remember. Bill, I told you to get the

midwife—"

"I did," he managed between panting breaths. "She tried but said to get you."

Mother Sarah drew the reins taut, halting Muley. "Already?"

Bill squatted, looking into Mother Sarah's eyes, color draining from his normally ruddy cheeks. "It's bad."

She massaged her temples, eyes squished shut. "How many times have I told you lads? Winterbourne does not mean born in winter!"

***

Mother Sarah marched into the Winterbourne household. Sylvia, Bill's wife, writhed on sweat-soaked linens, moaning, Marjorie the midwife nearby.

Sarah pulled Marjorie aside. "Breach?"

Marjorie crossed her arms. "Breach I can handle."

Sarah knelt before Sylvia, palpating her protruding belly.

"Maneuvers won't work," said Marjorie. Of course not. "Only one reason I'd call for you."

Mother Sarah bowed her head. "Understood." She stabbed a finger at Bill. "Find your sharpest knife."

Bill nodded and scurried away. Banging noises

emanated from the kitchen.

He emerged, wielding what could have passed for a short sword.

"Jam it in the fire," said Sarah.

He complied.

Sarah leaned forward, clasping Sylvia's clammy palms. "Listen. You must focus on an hour from now."

"This'll take an hour?" Sylvia spat through gritted teeth.

"No! No." Sarah softened her voice. "An hour from now, this will all be over. You'll have your baby and be completely healed."

"Healed?"

"Just focus on an hour from now." She turned to Bill. "The knife."

He whipped it from the fire, glowing red.

Sarah swiped it from him.

He staggered backwards, whimpering, pointing at the incandescent blade. "Why…?"

"Sanitation." Sarah shrugged. "And reduced blood loss."

"Blood loss…."

Bill collapsed.

WINTERBOURNE

Sarah glanced at Marjorie, jerking her head toward Bill. The midwife sauntered to his side.

With the burning blade in one hand, Sarah passed Sylvia an enormous chunk of tree bark with the other. "Between your teeth, please."

"Medicinal?" She grunted. "Pain relief?"

"Eh, more to keep you from biting through your tongue."

Sylvia swallowed and clamped down.

Sarah lifted Sylvia's gown, revealing her swollen abdomen, searing steel approaching. "Now think cool, wintry thoughts, Mrs. Winterbourne. It's about to get hot in here."

***

The last flock of migratory birds burst from a leafless tree beside the Winterbourne household, as if Sylvia's muffled scream was their cue to move on.

***

Sylvia sat beside Bill, across from Mother Sarah's desk at the church rectory, a newborn asleep in her arms.

Bill clutched his armrests, eyes down turned.

Sarah leaned back in her chair. "How are you, Sylvia? Any pain? Scars?"

Sylvia shook her head. "No. You were right. Completely healed."

"Such is the power of Claegg, Lord of the Land, Protector of the Harvest—well, you know the sermon."

The couple nodded.

"But I didn't call you over a day later to learn you were well. I was there…." She moved forward. "Bill?"

He looked up, as if no one had ever spoken to him before. "Yes?"

Sarah grinned. "Enjoying your birthday present?"

"Birthday…?"

"Yesterday?"

"Oh, yesterday was my birthday." His eyes fell on the baby. "Ha! Jill's my present. Funny."

"Already decided on a name? Wonderful. I hope, though, in the excitement, you didn't forget about your sister's birthday."

"Oh, right, yesterday—"

"Or your father's."

"Eh, yesterday—"

"Or your grandfather's, or Cousin Bob's, or—"

"Yes, all yesterday."

"In fact, everyone in your family was born on

the solstice."

"It's what makes us Winterbourne."

"Except that's not what your name means."

Bill's eyes turned downward. "You tell us that all the time."

"Yet no one listens. Another solstice, another Winterbourne."

Bill's eyes widened. "Jill's already a handful. We can't think about another—"

"And yet, you should. What if I had traveled a half-hour further before you tracked me down? We would have lost an entire hour."

"I thought you said half-hour?"

"Ugh. A half-hour to reach me, and a half-hour back. Poor Sylvia may not have had an hour left. Which is why I recommend Felg's Chant. Claegg understands sometimes a field should lie fallow."

"Excuse me," said Sylvia, "but am I the fallow field here?"

"Sorry, metaphors aren't my strong suit," said Sarah. "So, I'll be blunt. Sylvia, you may not survive the next Winterbourne, but this chant will prevent that."

The couple sat a little more upright.

"Is it—" Bill swallowed "—reversible?"

Sarah squinted. "Yes, it's reversible. As Claegg taketh, he can also giveth back. But—Sylvia!"

Their eyes locked. "Yes?"

Sarah splayed her arms on the desk like a panther about to pounce. "Yesterday, you saw your pink, pulsating womb emerge from a charred gash in your belly—your inner stomach flopped onto your outer stomach."

Sylvia's face blanched.

"Felg's Chant will prevent that. And you, Bill—don't pass out on me again."

Bill shook his head, blood recoloring his cheeks. "Sorry. 'Pulsating?'"

"A bit of an exaggeration, but the point's valid: this chant will protect you. Sylvia, you won't bear children, and Bill, you won't sire any."

"Me?"

"I need you both committed. Now join hands—oh, Sylvia, why don't you place Jill in the bassinet, if you plan on any grandchildren?"

Sylvia set the baby down and turned to Bill, joining hands.

"Good," said Sarah. "Are you ready?"

Sylvia nodded, glancing at Jill. "I just hope she doesn't grow up lonely."

"Now repeat after me…," started Sarah.

WINTERBOURNE

∗∗∗

Twelve Years Later

Mother Sarah entered Walter Shillington's dim bedroom. The old man lay in bed, family nearby. She addressed them. "So many well-wishers attending tonight gladdens me. Mrs. Shillington, Harry and Marry Shillington, your twins Barry and Carrie, so cute. Cousin Polly, and—uh, Jill?"

Jill Winterbourne beamed. "Yes, Mother Sarah?"

"You're here?"

"When I heard Mr. Shillington was dying, I figured you'd come to perform Last Rites."

Were the Shillingtons too polite to gasp? "And how long have you been here?"

"Oh, a half-hour maybe."

"Long enough to teach us all about the various worms and insects that devour a freshly buried corpse," said Marry. "A few years in, and I'm still learning my husband's religion. Such a knowledgeable assistant."

"Assistant, you say?" Sarah faced Jill. "That's how you introduced yourself? My assistant?"

Jill darted her eyes away.

Sarah bowed to the family. "I apologize, but Jill's enthusiasm for Claegg and his lore, eh, challenges one's patience." Her eyes found Jill's. "She means well, though." To the family she said,

Iowa [W]rites of Winter

"But I am here for a purpose. And, so, once again, Claegg calls another of his flock home…."

***

In the church's basement, Mother Sarah tended to Walter Shillington's body. Jill stood in the corner.

Sarah did not look up. "Jill, go home."

"I want to help prepare Mr. Shillington."

"You're too young."

"I read all about how."

"Then read some more."

"I've already read all the books on the bottom shelf. Last Rites. Baby Births and What Can Go Wrong. Harvest Blessings. The Healing Arts. Crop Diseases and How to Treat Them. Animal Husbandry. Animal Wifery—everything. Twice."

"You made up that last one."

"Well, it should exist."

"And the upper shelf—"

"No, I haven't touched any of Clerics in Peril: Adventures of Claegg's Chosen Warriors, Volumes I through XI."

Sarah leaned on the table, glancing over her shoulder. "But why so much reading? Just play with the other farmers' kids."

"Everyone's too spread out." Jill looked Mother Sarah in the eyes. "You're closer."

Should she...? Sarah shook her head. "You're just too young. Go upstairs, pick a book, and re-reread it." Too soon, too young, but... "And leave Clerics in Peril alone. I'll know if you don't."

***

Jill skulked upstairs and plopped in a chair facing the bookshelves.

Each book appeared equally thick.

Obviously, whoever wrote these used the same blank books, gradually filling them out.

She approached the shelves, eyes gliding along the upper tomes. No one could miss the gap she'd leave if she pulled, say, Volume VII. But, if Crop Diseases somehow sneaked in there by mistake....

TWO: Ingrid

Ingrid sat at the card table in her friend Howie's basement, admiring the dungeon map he had hand drawn. "When're the others arriving?"

Howie scrolled through his text messages across from her. "They haven't replied."

Ingrid glanced at the gray haze from the egress window, blinking colorful lights seeping through the edges of the front yard display. "Better show up quick, or they'll get snowed out."

"Why? So they can derail the main quest by stealing an NPC's weapon and running? Or adopting another goblin mascot?"

"Hey, Squamsquat is a valuable addition to the team, and you have to admit, you love doing her voice."

Sounding somewhere between Grover and Elmo, Howie muttered, "'Pat my head for a penny?'"

They stared at each other and burst out laughing.

Howie settled,eyes darting from side to side, as if someone might pop in by surprise. "While we wait, I have something for you." He passed her a small, gift-wrapped box.

She weighed it in her hand. "Got some heft. Uh, the others…?"

Did Howie blush? "No, no. It's just for you."

"Yeah, wouldn't want to make them jealous." Ingrid tore it open.

Inside the box lay a metallic 20-sided die an inch-and-a-half across.

Howie covered his grinning face. "It's titanium."

Ingrid rolled it around in her palm, marveling at it. "Feels heavier than a water bottle, but…" colorful highlights along the edges contrasted from the dark gray metal "…seems lighter than it should."

"Titanium's light!" said Howie, a little too loudly. "I mean, lighter than steel. But almost as strong."

Ingrid suppressed a sob and bear-hugged him. "Oh, Howie!" she said, voice muffled in his sweater. She released him. "Let's try it out! 11 or higher, our friends show up, 10 or less, they don't."

She flung it on the table, but it bounced off, rolling to a stop by a closet door, ajar.

A dark flicker appeared to swipe it inside the closet.

Ingrid blinked. "Did you see that?"

Howie frowned, paling slightly.

Ingrid tiptoed to the door and, in one move, swung it open.

The die sat in the middle of the closet floor.

Ingrid sighed. "A natural 1. I guess it's just us tonight." She leaned to pick it up.

The closet door slammed shut, plunging her into darkness.

"Ha, ha, Howie." Ingrid clasped the doorknob, rattling it. "C'mon, this isn't like—"

Doorknob, door, darkness—all vanished.

White blinding light engulfed her.

Eyes adjusting, she found herself on a snow-covered slope, pines and firs dotting the landscape.

Three black-cloaked women stood before her, one young, one middle-aged, and one who was neither.

Ingrid gasped, covering her mouth. "Witches!" She squinted. "A coven of witches?"

The witches regarded each other. The young one started, "How?"

Ingrid pointed at her. "You're the maiden." To the middle-aged witch, "You're the mother." To the third, "And you're the haaaaa—uh, croooo—uh, the third one."

The Third One, hooded, not be-hatted like the others, nodded, but her ancient purplish complexion, pointy ears protruding between stark white locks, belied few wrinkles.

"Wow," said Ingrid, "you're a dark elf!"

The Maiden started again, "How?"

The Mother cut her off with a raised hand, addressing Ingrid. "Please excuse her. We rarely get this kind of reaction."

A cold breeze reminded Ingrid of her coat draped over Howie's chair. "Where am I?"

The Mother spread her arms. "You have found yourself within the realm of Upper Claegg. Unseen forces have chosen you—"

"I'm the chosen one?"

The Maiden scowled, motioning toward Ingrid.

The Mother raised her hand again. "Our friend here seems knowledgeable of our ways. Yes, Ingrid, you are among the chosen, but the chosen one?"

The Third One pierced Ingrid's soul with a penetrating, golden-eyed stare. "Only time will tell."

Ingrid gulped.

The Maiden glanced over her shoulder. "They'll be here soon."

"Who?" asked Ingrid.

"A squadron of orcs who patrol this area," said The Mother.

"Orcs? Are we talking, like, people-eating chaotic-evil-all-the-time orcs, or nuanced, not-a-monolith, playable character, modern orcs?"

The Maiden scowled. "What are you talking about? They're just orcs." She raised her hand to her ear, grinning evilly. "Hear the clinking metal as they march? Won't be long now."

"What am I supposed to do? I can't fight. I have no weapons or armor." Ingrid shivered. "I don't even have a coat."

"For now," said The Mother, "follow their lead. They'll take you to their camp, where more of your kind wait."

"An entire camp of chosen ones? Why, to battle it out, Hunger Games-style, revealing the chosen?"

The Third One grunt-chuckled. "You catch on fast."

The clinking metal grew louder.

Ingrid looked around frantically. "I can't do this, not for real. I gotta get out of here."

"My child—" started The Mother.

Ingrid jabbed a finger at her. "I am not your child. And I'm 15."

The Mother began again. "Slightly-older-not-my-child, the picture my associates enjoy painting is not as dire as it seems. The orcs will provide for you at the camp, as they must, while you get your bearings. You shall find your place in this realm."

"No! Just send me home, now!"

The Third One laughed. "What kind of adventurer refuses her quest?"

Quest?

The Third One held a crystal-topped walking staff, while the other two, brooms—except, The Maiden wasn't so much holding her broom, as steadying it on its bristles, inches deep in the snow, the tip of her finger on the tip of the handle.

Derail the quest.

"Witches be crazy!" With a growl that

shocked even herself, Ingrid rushed The Maiden, swiped her broom, hopped on it, and sped away into the snow-covered forest.

***

The Third One erupted into a belly laugh.

The Maiden sulked. "How am I supposed to fly back now?"

"Ride with me, deary," said The Mother.

The Third One wiped a tear from her eye. "'Witches be crazy.'"

***

Trees and mist thickened as Ingrid flew down the slope, every branch seeming to smack her in the face. She rose above the treetops, but the wind picked up, slashing her exposed arms with prickles of ice and snow.

A blizzard was forming.

Slowing down could cut the wind chill but also trap her in this cold even longer.

Gritting her teeth, feeling leaving her broom-gripped fingers (long lost from her toes), moisture in her nose and eyes freezing, she pressed through a clearing.

A light in the distance! She focused on it, the blurring snow intensifying.

***

The Winterbournes jumped at the door-rattling crash. Jill looked from her book to her father.

Bill approached the door, slowly swinging it open.

A girl with a broom lay on their threshold.

Sylvia rushed past Bill and knelt by the child. "You poor baby."

The girl reached up, blood trickling from her scalp, eyes locking on Jill. "How…." She collapsed.

THREE: Sisterhood

Ingrid awoke in a bed a little too small for her, thick blankets tucked under her arms, feet protruding like tips of Iceberg Ingrid, floating on the Duvet Sea. An older woman with curly gray locks hovered over her. She palpated Ingrid's toes.

"Warmth returning." She grasped Ingrid's hands. "The same." She faced a pair of adults Ingrid suddenly realized were also standing in the room. "The frostbite's cured. She'll need more rest for the head wound."

"Head wound?" Ingrid touched her forehead.

Shards of white pain exploded behind her eyes.

Ingrid arched her back, heaving.

"Here child." Gray Locks reached for Ingrid's head, fingertips glowing—glowing?

"No," whispered Ingrid, closing her eyes. "Hurts…," but she couldn't summon the strength to resist.

Warm fingers pressed against Ingrid's temples. The urge to wince dissipated, along with the residual white shards. She felt stronger, more awake. She sat up, but Gray Locks stopped her.

"Rest, child. Head wounds are always tricky, and you left a splintered dent on their door. I could waste a lot of healing energy, missing the core injury, so rest is essential."

Ingrid settled back into bed. "Okay, but who are you?" She squinted at Gray Locks' white square on her black collar. "Are you a priest—ess?"

"Priest. Pastor. Most just call me Mother Sarah."

"You healed me? You can do that?"

"Such is the power of Our Lord Claegg."

Half-formed jokes about religion and health care systems bubbled through Ingrid's brain, but the connections never solidified. "Thanks," she muttered.

"I'll leave you two while I speak with the Winterbournes."

"Two?"

At the foot of the bed, a pair of tween-age eyes fixated on her.

"Uh, hello?"

The brown-haired girl rushed to her bedside. "I'm Jill Winterbourne, and this is my room."

"Thanks for letting me—"

"I help Mother Sarah."

"You're her assistant?"

Jill looked sideways. "I assist her."

"Well, maybe you can assist me. She said to rest, but when she healed my head, it wired me."

"Wired?"

"Uh, woke me up, so I can't rest now."

Jill gasped. "I've got it!" She crouched, tiptoeing to the door, nudging it until it latched, cutting off the adults' already muffled discussion.

She scrambled to the bedside, reached under it, and produced a thick volume. "I'll read to you." She leaned in. "But it has to be a secret."

Ingrid nodded, squinting to suppress the flickering-white discomfort nipping at her temples. "Easy enough, but why?"

Jill glanced at the closed door. "Mother Sarah said I mustn't read Clerics in Peril until I'm older."

"Won't she notice it's missing?"

WINTERBOURNE

"She didn't for volumes I through VI."

***

Mother Sarah slid the door ajar as she left Jill's bedroom. To the adult Winterbournes: "I believe another day of rest should bring your unexpected guest back to full health."

"Good to hear," said Sylvia.

"But we have a prob—" started Bill.

Sarah raised her finger, eyes sideways toward the door.

It slowly latched shut.

"Sorry, Bill," said Sarah. "Please continue."

"We're stocked enough for the winter to feed three." Bill let the last word linger.

"And?" said Sarah, feigning ignorance.

"Are you going to bring this poor girl to live with you, or is this new mouth to feed our—?"

"Shh," said Sylvia, patting Bill on the chest. To Sarah: "I'm sure we'll manage, and if we must tighten our belts, or—" she eyed Bill up and down "—suspenders, so be it."

"Good to hear," said Sarah, wrapping herself in her coat (and, this time, itchy scarf), "especially from the head of the most prosperous farm this season." She strode to the door, grasping the knob. "As always, the church keeps its own provisions for those in need, so if you truly need anything, don't hesitate to ask." She left.

***

Jill regaled Ingrid with the Clerics in Peril series, and Ingrid regaled Jill with tales of life on Earth, going to pains explaining that her tabletop adventures were not real (although Jill never fully understood). Meanwhile, the family managed on their winter rations, consuming much smaller portions than Ingrid was used to.

Although she had lost weight on her winter ration diet, Ingrid's above-average Earth height towered over most villagers. Chaddy, the blacksmith, normally unaccustomed to working with women, dared not object when Ingrid walked in asking for a job.

Jill assisted Mother Sarah to the point she relented, finally introducing her to others as "my assistant."

Seasonal fairs came and went, Ingrid vending the wares she and Chaddy forged, Jill assisting Mother Sarah with the occasional heat stroke or archery mishap. At the close of each day, the would-be sisters squeezed into Jill's cramped bedroom, regaling each other once more.

***

"…and that's what they call a montage scene in movies," said Ingrid.

"Wow," said Jill. "I didn't understand any of that."

"I could show you if my phone still worked."

"Oorth is so strange."

"'Earth,' and, yeah, you don't know the half of it."

Jill watched Ingrid, sitting on the edge of the bed her father built and crammed into their bedroom. She had paid close attention to Ingrid's reaction while telling her tales from Volume VIII, featuring Maria de Westend, famed for renouncing her royal lineage as princess, joining the church of the common folk. Rumors flew about Maria's steadfast companion Ophelia, but the cleric's personal writings in Volume VIII made explicit what everyone had suspected. Ingrid just shrugged, though, mentioning a similar warrior princess, residing somewhere on Earth called "Teevee."

Would Ingrid understand these feelings growing inside Jill over the past year? She never told Mother Sarah why she stopped playing with the other farm girls—and never would—fearing the ridicule after planting a sloppy smooch on her then best friend Leda at age eleven. But Maria served Our Lord Claegg while living this lifestyle, so the Protector of the Harvest wouldn't mind, right? And Ingrid...?

Jill visualized sidling next to her, stroking her hair, whispering in her—

"What?" asked Ingrid.

Jill realized how long she had been staring. "Uh, sorry."

"Eh, don't worry. We all space off. By the way, do you think something will interrupt Mother

Sarah's winter sojourn again? I mean, none of your relatives are pregnant, but it is the winter solstice, so—"

"Ingrid, I have to tell you something." She surprised herself by standing to say this.

Ingrid leaned back but smiled. "Uh, okay."

That word again. "Remember the story I was telling you?"

"Milgrim, the Grim Miller-Turned-Grim-Warrior of Claegg from Volume X?"

"No, before that."

"Sasha, Queen of Moles—"

"That was Volume VI. I'm talking about Maria? De Westend?"

"Oh, the warrior princess. What about her?"

"Well, her tale—"

A crash resounded from the front door.

Ingrid and Jill burst into the den, finding splintered wood on the floor.

The doorknob rattled.

Ingrid reached for it, but Bill intervened. "Step aside."

Jill whispered, "You were going to open the door?"

"Sure," she said, "to protect you."

Jill placed her hands on her heart, blushing, "Ingrid, I—"

"Stand back!" Bill flung the door wide open.

A tall stocky boy hopped inside, holding something in his hand, cold air rushing in from behind him. "Stand back—did someone already say that?" He shook his head and waved the thing around. "I hold an object of immense power, and—"

"Howie!" Ingrid rushed the boy, lifting him with a bear hug.

Tears streaming, Howie broke away. "We must go now, so the witches can send us back home!"

Ingrid gaped. "Back? For real?"

"Just hop on this broom with me."

"And your 'immense power' thing?"

"Oh! They said you dropped this."

In his hand sat the titanium 20-sided die.

Ingrid grasped him again, kissing him on the lips. Both bodies relaxed into the embrace.

She leaned back, blushing, and rubbed the top of his head. "A helmet?"

"The witches said I'd need it."

Remnants of the front door collapsed off

their hinges.

***

Leda all over again. The ridicule. The laughing. At least Jill hadn't ventured so far out on a limb this time. She tried to slink away, but Ingrid broke from Howie. "Wait, you need to meet Jill."

"We don't have time," said Howie.

"But Jill's been reading me these adventures." She grasped Jill's hand, pulling her closer. "They're the adventures we've been pretending to have."

"So?"

"In this realm, we could adventure—for real."

Howie stood still, speechless.

"All right." Ingrid lifted the die from Howie's hand. "11 or higher we stay, 10 or less, we go."

Howie swallowed and nodded.

Ingrid handed it to Jill. "Would you do the honors?"

Jill clasped it to her heart. "What now?"

"Just drop it."

Jill held the die out and released.

It bounced and tumbled, rolling to a stop.

Ingrid grinned. "Nat twenty."

***

Waiting in the frigid mountain air, The Third One gazed into her staff's clairvoyant crystal, taking in the Ingrid-Howie reunion. "Good!"

"We still have to deal with those know-it-alls," said The Maiden, peeking over The Third One's shoulder. "How is that good?"

The Mother shrugged. "We didn't know how to send them back, anyway."

FOUR: Solitude

Mother Sarah, hunkering in the icy wind, snapped the reins. "Move it, Muley."

Maybe this year she would complete her two-day sojourn, reaching her sister's cottage on the balmier west coast, without interruption. But even Muley's top speed (about the same as his average and slow speeds) couldn't out-pace the approaching footsteps.

Sarah turned toward the interloper. "Bill—Jill?"

She tugged Muley's reins to a halt.

"Your mule—?"

"Yes, Muley. What's the matter, child?"

Jill caught her breath. "I want to become a Chosen Warrior of Claegg."

Mother Sarah eyed Jill up and down. "What did I tell you about reading Clerics in Peril?"

Jill raised her hand to her mouth. "You knew?"

"I warned you I would."

***

Howie rented a room above a bakery, paid for by working at said bakery. Meanwhile, Ingrid honed her craft, surprising her friends with their own bespoke armor sets.

"Why me?" asked Jill.

"You'll need it as a Chosen Warrior," said Ingrid.

"But I'm just starting."

"And you'll have a leg up on the others, already clad in armor."

"When do you go away?" asked Howie.

"Next month," said Jill.

"An entire month to get used to walking around in your new armor," said Ingrid. "I made myself a set, too, so we could all roam the village as armor buddies."

Jill chuckled. "Aren't you afraid we'll look dumb?"

"Who cares?" said Howie. "We'll be off adventuring soon, and you're going to your clerical monastery, or whatever."

"For how long?" asked Ingrid.

Jill looked down. "Two years."

"Wow. And none of us can visit you?"

Jill shook her head.

"Then let's make this month count."

***

After an eventful month that could have filled its own montage, Jill, Ingrid, and Howie marched toward the covered wagon at the end of the street. Two Claegg-Chosen hopefuls, draped in standard peasant garb, stared from within, agape, as Jill, armor clad, massive mace over her shoulder, approached them.

She turned to her friends, sniffling. "I guess this is it."

"C'mere, you." Ingrid drew her into an enormous hug, armor scraping against armor.

The kids in the wagon covered their ears.

Jill disengaged and spread her arms toward Howie, settling on a simple handshake, gauntlets crunching together. "So good to meet you."

"Likewise," he said.

Jill bit her lip, eyes sideways on Ingrid. Would she really leave it like this? How long could she keep this burden to herself? "Ingrid." She steadied her breathing. "I love you."

Ingrid beamed. "Aw, I love you, too!" She moved in for another hug, but her head passed Jill's, burrowing into her shoulder. Ingrid pulled away. "The little sister I never had."

Jill hoped no one noticed her pursed lips. She forced a smile. "Right back atcha, Big Sis."

"Howie!" said Ingrid.

Howie looked up. "Hmm?"

"You're using your phone?"

He showed them a large crystal attached to the back. "I met a guy. No bars or anything, but I can do this." He raised it, motioning for the three of them to move in closer. "Selfie time. On three, one—three!"

It clicked with a flash.

Jill blinked her eyes. "What just happened?"

"Check it out." He showed her the image. "Now the three of us can stay together forever."

"Yeah," said Ingrid, "until you accidentally smash the screen on a rock."

"I met a guy for that, too."

Together, forever, all three of them. Three. "Well, I better go." Jill climbed onto the wagon.

The kids scampered deeper within, giving her a wide berth.

WINTERBOURNE

Jill watched Ingrid and Howie wave to her, arms over each other's shoulders, as the wagon wobbled away. She waved back until the landscape swallowed them up. With a heavy sigh, she placed her face in her hands and wept.

***

Ingrid and Howie waved until the wagon disappeared behind a hill.

"Nice save with the sisterly love, by the way," said Howie.

"Yeah." Ingrid wrapped her arm around Howie's waist, pressing her cheek against his. "She'll meet the right girl someday."

Won't she?

Epilogue

Mother Sarah marveled at how Muley pulled this wagon weighed down with kids at the same speed as her own much lighter cart. A farmer—the quintessential farmer, appearing exactly as one would imagine upon hearing "a farmer"—sat beside her.

"Jill Winterbourne has come a long way since her perilous birth," said Sarah.

The farmer puffed from his pipe. "Winterbourne, 'edge of winter.' No wonder they're all born on the solstice."

"Hush," said Sarah. "They don't know that."

"If'n they did—" perfect smoke rings danced from his mouth "—maybe some'd be born on the equinox."

"What about the streams, drying up in summer?"

"Them's winterbournes, completely different."

"As you say, Claegg."

The Defeat of Winter

Jill Cronbaugh

The slender icicle queen
stands majestically
watching her winter kingdom.
Her jester snowflakes amuse her no longer.
Her monarchy crumbles under
the invading sun.
She
slowly
but
regally
a
b
d
i
c
a
t
e
s
.

The Snow Queen's Apprentice

JE Brooke

The silver hand-mirror shattered into dozens of pieces on the unforgiving cobbles, shocking the watching crowd into silence. Gerda lifted her head, letting the silence wash over her and sweep away the last of the noise from clawing into her brain. That had been the point of destroying the mirror, she supposed; to stop the laughing, the jeers, as the girls tried to show her what they had done to her face.

***

The group of girls had approached offering friendship. She shouldn't have trusted it, had years of experience that should have taught her what such overtures usually meant. They hadn't given her much of a choice, though. They'd surrounded her and sat her down on the low wall of the school garden, pulling out paints, brushes, and rouges from their pockets, smearing them thickly over her skin. The attack went on forever. Gerda's skin crawled under the rough brushes, hair pulling, and the ceaseless giggling. She could see between the girls that a crowd of other students was starting to gather, curious and watching. They drew closer as the circle of girls stopped their ministrations and stepped back. One of them held a mirror out for her to see what they had done.

Gerda took it in shaking hands and lifted it

until she could see her reflection. A stranger looked back; not beautiful but garish, the makeup applied hurriedly and without the skill she knew they had. The girls encircling her always looked lovely, something Gerda had never managed to master for herself. They smirked and cooed "Oh, Gerda, don't you look pretty!" in tones that she had long ago learned were mocking. Frantically, she scanned the approaching crowd of students— already jeering at her expense—for Kai, but he hung back from her like he had since the beginning of the term.

They'd been friends since infancy, after their respective parents had died in the same epidemic. Before, he'd never seemed to mind how she could sometimes go quiet and strange, how sometimes she could lose hours in a book or the garden without realizing, or how she could talk about a subject that interested her for hours without tiring or realizing that others were bored. None of those things had mattered, until they had started this term, and Kai had found himself popular with the rest of the students, while Gerda found herself on the outside as always. He'd distanced himself from her, purposefully ignored her when she tried to talk to him, now that he had other, more interesting friends to spend time with.

The laughter from the students swelled and crashed over her, drowning her in noise that crawled under her skin, up her spine, and over her brain. She'd give anything to make the noise, the attention, the jagged perception, stop. Without thinking, she raised the mirror still in her hands and smashed it on the ground; fractured slivers of glass scattered on the cobbles or briefly became airborne. Gerda yelped at a sharp pain in her left eye. Had one of the fragments been thrown that high? It seemed impossible, but the burn said otherwise. Fighting every instinct to rub her injured eye, she barely discerned the owner of the mirror shout angrily, "That was a family heirloom, you little troll! You're going to pay for the damage that you've done!"

"What's going on over here?" One of the teachers' voices broke over the din.

"It was Gerda, ma'am!" the owner of the mirror began, suddenly distraught. "She broke my-"

The girl was cut short by a cold, driving gust of wind. Gerda hunched over, gingerly covering her eye to protect it from further harm. Bracing for the gust to end and the punishment for breaking the mirror to begin. But the wind didn't stop. Instead, it only grew in ferocity and began to carry increasing swarms of snow into the faces in the gathered crowd.

"Everyone inside, now!" the teacher shouted, and the other students clamored to get back in the warm safety of the school house. Gerda stayed where she was, paralyzed by the burn in her eye and the freezing wind. And then, as suddenly as they had begun, they stopped.

Gerda slowly uncurled herself out of her hunch, uncovered her eye and started to look around the now-vacant schoolyard. Nearly vacant, it turned out. A woman dressed in white furs sat in a white and silver sledge trimmed with evergreen boughs and pulled by two large, well-groomed reindeer. The air around them seemed frozen by the woman's cool gaze as it bored directly into Gerda's heart.

The Snow Queen's Apprentice

"Come with me, if you wish," the woman said quietly, but the crisp sound of her voice carried much farther than it should have over the empty yard.

Gerda's words left her, as they sometimes did when she was overwhelmed. But her feet evidently had her reply as they slowly moved toward the sledge, then up and onto the rear seat behind the frozen woman. The woman - the queen, for could she be anything else with her crown of ice - turned to face Gerda, and reached down to hand her a thick blanket to wrap herself in. The queen snapped the reins in her hands. The snow and wind began to howl again, and the reindeer leapt into the sky and away from the only village Gerda had known her whole life.

***

Almost as soon as she began shivering in the frigid evening air, the thumbnail moon beginning its ascent into the darkening sky, the queen took something from the front seat of the sledge and handed it to Gerda. "Wrap this around yourself, child." Another blanket, large enough to wrap around her whole body several times was charmed with a comforting weight. The mottled white, black, and gray fibers looked new, but were as soft on her skin as if they'd been worn with the passage of many years. She pulled the blanket tight around herself and buried her face in the warmth, releasing a long breath.

"Thank you," Gerda said, her voice returned at last. She didn't know, though, if it would carry to the other woman over the wind rushing past them as they flew.

"You called to me," the queen said again, not turning around.

"For that," Gerda replied. "And for the blanket. How did I call you?"

"Through the mirror. I saw your distress through the shard that went into your eye."

A family heirloom, the girl had said after Gerda smashed it. Certainly old enough to have some kind of enchantment.

"Where are we going?"

"Where do you want to go?"

"I-I don't know. Just not back." Not to the school, not to the not-quite-kind girls. Not to Kai and his silence. Not ever.

"Would you like to come to my home? It's very cold, but beautiful. And quiet."

Quiet. Gerda wanted to wrap herself in quiet like the blanket. And maybe the blanket around her would keep out the rest of the cold.

"Yes."

***

The queen had told her there would be cold. She hadn't said there would be warmth as well. Or comfort. Gerda let the blanket fall to the worn oak floors of the cabin as they stepped into the foyer. The queen walked ahead toward the roaring fire in the large stone hearth. Gerda jogged to catch up, meeting her host in a large open room with windows that went all the way up to the ceiling. The large house overlooked rolling snow-covered plains. The dark shapes of reindeer, oxen, and other animals moved beneath ribbons of color that split the sky at random, breathtaking intervals. She'd seen something like them in her village, but never this vibrant. Too many other lights shined too brightly.

"We see them most nights here," the queen said, seeing Gerda's awe and delight. She went to a large cauldron on the fireplace and ladled something piping hot into a bowl, then offered it to her. Gerda took it hesitantly. The stew, thick and creamy white, smelled delicious. Nervous that the texture and taste would mean she wouldn't be able to eat it, she raised the bowl to her lips and took a tentative sip. A delicious medley of potatoes, leeks, cream, and tender stewed meat washed over her tongue; smooth and nourishing and warm. The rest was gone in moments. The queen didn't smile, but Gerda thought her eyes didn't seem as cold as before. She hoped that meant she was pleased.

"What do I call you?"

"Gerda. What should I call you?"

"You may call me Skare. Would you like more?"

It didn't take long for Skare's cabin to feel like home. Many days and nights Gerda spent exploring every inch of the expansive house. Gerda's room was larger than the dorm she had shared with a dozen other children, and she had it all to herself! Every morning she rose from the soft, warm bed, slipped on her flannel-lined house shoes and went to meet Skare for breakfast before the queen went out to tend and manage her reindeer herds.

Once Skare had left, Gerda spun around the house, roaming the halls until she knew every nook and cranny like the back of her hand, investigating the strange and wondrous artifacts that she found. The most magnificent curio was an enormous gilt-silver mirror propped against a wall in the hallway. The first time she walked past it, her reflection lasted a moment before fading into a fractal pattern of broken blue and white sky, slate and straw roofs that looked all-too familiar poking into the periphery. Startled, she careened back into the wall behind her, wincing as she slammed her elbows into the hard surface. That night, once the shock subsided and gave way to curiosity, she asked Skare about it.

"The mirror you shattered was one of its siblings. There are many around the world, made long ago. Most of their owners have forgotten the magic they contain and see them only as relics and heirlooms passed down through generations," the queen told her over their dinner. The ethereal lights in the sky were partially blocked by dense clouds that night, and the occasional snow flurry drifted down to be illuminated by the lights in the cabin window.

Gerda stared down at her bowl and nudged her food around, overcome by guilt. If the mirror was special, and powerful, she shouldn't have broken it. Another thing she had gotten wrong. Suddenly, a large hand was on hers. Gerda looked up and met Skare's cool gaze.

"I am glad that you broke it," Skare said. "It

had not been of use to anyone for generations, and through it I was able to help you."

"Had anyone ever used it to call you before?"

"No. But I used one to call the being who brought me here."

***

Gerda avoided the mirror for the next few days, until curiosity won out. She stood in front of it again. After a moment. there was a ripple and she could see through the mirror shard forgotten in the square of her school. The sky was clear and unbroken blue this time, and at the edges of the portal she could see the eves of the surrounding buildings had recently accumulated several inches of snow. The ground, however, must have been cleared, for nothing obscured the portal itself. Or maybe that was part of the mirror's enchantment. She watched the scene for a moment and then started to move on, but a movement through the portal caught her eye. The sky was moving. No, that wasn't right. The shard was being moved, lifted into the air. The rough and jangling motion sent a wave of nausea rolling through her, but then it steadied as it was hoisted to its new owner's face. Gerda gasped softly as Kai's face came into view.

***

Skare had once come from human lands, although the snow queen couldn't remember how long ago precisely. Her story had been much the same as Gerda's: no family to speak of, different in ways that set her apart from the others in her village. Marked her as strange, to be avoided or ridiculed. Skare said she'd found the large silver mirror that now hung in the cabin in a disused barn she'd used to hide in one day. She'd been so desperate to escape her pursuers in the village, that the sheer force of her desire echoed through the mirror and called to someone Skare only referred to as Aster. She'd stayed with Aster in their realm for a time, but found she was better suited to the work and climate of the far north. Her guardian had found her this place to tend, and it sounded to Gerda like there was still regular contact between them.

***

Kai put the mirror shard on a shelf in his dorm bookcase. Sometimes Gerda watched him as he moved about the small room. Sometimes she didn't. Occasionally, when she watched, Kai would stop whatever he was doing, look over to the shard, and stare at it for a long time. At first, Gerda wondered if he could see her peering out at him, but eventually she concluded that he was lost in his own thoughts. The corners of his mouth were pulled down when he looked at it. Once, tears welled in his eyes and overflowed. Anger boiled in Gerda as she watched her former friend break down looking at the mirror fragment. She clenched her fists, stalked down the hall, and didn't stop back again for a long, long time.

Eventually, she started helping Skare with the reindeer herds; mucking out stalls, feeding them, brushing them and polishing their harnesses. There was something soothing about working with the animals, even if she didn't take to it as naturally as Skare seemed to do. Still, the creatures didn't seem to mind her presence, and there was no pressure to talk or put on any kind of a performance. All that was required was calm, quiet, and concentration, and that Gerda could provide. Skare was a good mentor, and she was animated around the herd in a way that Gerda had never seen before. It was almost as though the rest of the world disappeared when she was with them, and as she watched, Gerda wished with all her heart that she could find something to be as passionate about. Skare apparently recognized the longing Gerda felt, because before long, the queen informed Gerda that they were going to visit Aster.

***

Gerda hadn't been back in the sledge since leaving her home village. It seemed smaller, after so much time had passed. The trip from Skare's realm passed quickly and soon the weather warmed enough that she had to strip some of the layers back that were necessary living in perpetual snow and ice. Tundra gave way to vast forests and, shockingly, gardens.

"Who tends all of these?" Gerda shouted over the wind.

"Aster does," Skare said without looking away from their present course. "As well as the gardeners she trains."

They landed on a broad tile pavilion surrounded by what seemed from the ground like endless fields of roses, bursting with blooms in impossibly bright hues. The air was thick with birdsong and sunshine, jarring after the quiet cold and darkness she had grown to love so much. As she adjusted to the clamor, the figure of an old woman approached, dressed in loose clothes adorned with large splotches of dirt at the knees and sleeves and wearing a wide brimmed straw hat. Skare strode forward to meet her friend and, much to Gerda's surprise, embraced her.

"It's wonderful to see you, my dear," the old woman, presumably Aster, said as she released her former charge. "I'm glad you could find time to visit."

"I will always make time to see you, my friend," Skare replied, lips pulling into as much of a smile as Gerda had ever seen.

"And this must be your assistant!" Aster said, turning to Gerda herself. She fought the instinct to shy away.

"My name is Gerda," she said shakily, despite having rehearsed the introduction hundreds of times in her head on the way over.

"Lovely to meet you, Gerda. Why don't you both come with me? I have lunch prepared for you after your journey."

The meal was delicious, and after, Aster led them on a tour of the surrounding rose gardens. Their pace along the crushed stone path was relaxed and ambling. Gerda soaked in the sun and enjoyed the warm breeze caressing her face. They stopped by a young man crouched at the base of a rose bush so large it could have been mistaken for a tree. "Good afternoon, Niko. How is your patient doing?"

The young man kept working for a moment and didn't acknowledge that he had been spoken to. Then, he reached to his side,grasped the handle of a long, tapered stick, and etched words into the dirt by the plant.

The mites seem under control. There's no new stippling. Your advice worked.

"Excellent, Niko, I'm glad! Let me know if I can be of any more use."

Niko nodded, continuing with his work, and they continued their walk.

***

Visits to Aster, Niko, and the gardens became a regular part of Gerda and Skare's routine. It became as comforting and familiar to Gerda as tending the reindeer, or reading, or gaming with Skare to relax in the evenings. Each time, Aster showed them different parts of her grounds, different flowers and herbs and orchards. Sometimes Niko came with them, sometimes he did not. He never spoke audibly when he was with them, but he always carried either his baton for etching in the earth or a small slate and piece of chalk. But he was kind, attentive, and more than happy to provide information about the gardens and answer Gerda's questions. Sometimes, there was a hesitance in his scribbling hand, like he was suddenly afraid he'd gone on too long, that he'd bored her. She knew that experience too well.

One visit, after mentioning she had a headache, Aster handed her a mug of tea and told her to drink. She felt better afterward, and asked what was in it. Aster deferred to Niko to explain. He launched into an explanation of the different kinds of medicinal properties of the plants they tended. Gerda was rapt, and barely noticed any time at all had passed until Skare put a cool, gentle hand on her shoulder and told her it was time to go home. Aster must have seen her disappointment, for she slipped a small volume into Gerda's hands on healing plants and told her to read for next time. Gerda almost missed the slight upward draw of Skare's lips; would have, if she hadn't known what to look for.

***

"How long have you trained under Aster?"

I'm not sure. She found me when I was little. I grew up among these gardens and decided I wanted to learn how to care for them. Aster trained me, but she's basically my mother. What about you and Skare?

"The same. She saved me; helped me when I was younger. I can't imagine my life anywhere else."

Would you ever want to?

***

Gerda was consumed. She devoured books and knowledge and lessons on healing plants, the powers they possessed. The magic she could wield through them. She still enjoyed the reindeer and books and games with Skare, but her lessons with Aster and Niko were mesmerizing. Her room was filled with plants in pots and jars of lush earth and dried samples, mortars and pestles and tomes on healing. Such knowledge at her fingertips. Knowledge, perhaps, that could have saved her parents. Or Kai's.

The Snow Queen's Apprentice

***

With her studies and chores and time spent in the company of Skare, Aster, and Niko, she couldn't remember the last time she had been to visit the mirror. The shard was in a different room now, although it still belonged to a child, toys and picture books stacked in a corner not far from where the child slept. Light flooded in through the windows, and still the child in the bed slept. An adult came into the room, his back turned to the shard at first as he stood over the child in the bed. He rubbed a hand over his face, shoulders held stiff. A woman and the wizened version of someone Gerda recognized as the village doctor came into the room and stood over the child as well. The doctor carefully examined his young patient, whose chest rose and fell raggedly when exposed to the open air, occasionally shuddering in a clear labored cough. The doctor's face was grave, and lined with weariness beyond his age. A cold knot of dread settled in Gerda's stomach, as he rose and left the room after a brief word to the parents. The woman collapsed into the man's arms, and he now stood in full view of the shard's gaze. He was older, certainly, but still recognizable. For a moment, he looked sorrowfully at the mirror fragment he had carried and cared for for so many years, and then over to the bed where his sick child lay clinging to life. Finally breaking, he buried his face in the woman's shoulder and joined her weeping.

***

They never talked about her old village. There was no point. Gerda didn't want to go back, she was happy with Skare, and her studies, and the reindeer, and Niko and Aster. She still didn't want

125

to go back. But now - she had lost track of time.

Gerda had seen that look on the doctor's face once before, when she was a small girl and there had been an outbreak of sickness among the children of the village. Gerda and Kai had recovered after only a brief illness. But others - others were not so lucky. The doctor, much younger then, had been called to help but could ultimately do nothing besides provide some comfort to those who would never get better. Gerda had watched from her recovery room, had seen that same look on the doctor's face. She hadn't recognized the expression then, but she knew what she saw now: futility. There was nothing that the village doctor could do for Kai's child or any of the other children who were probably in the same state, if the last epidemic had been any indication. There was nothing anyone still living in mortal lands could do, and so it was left to Gerda.

She could have been angry. The part of her that had been the scared and lonely little girl was still angry. But that was only one part of her now. The Gerda she was now grieved with that child, felt her pain and acknowledged it as she slipped on her coat and lined boots and walked out into the long arctic night with her specimen bag slung over her shoulder.

Gerda had found the cure a few months before, pouring through a new text from Aster without any real purpose other than absorbing the information. She'd noted it at the time with mild curiosity, and then moved on. She didn't know if the cure had been lost to humanity, or if it had ever only been known to beings like Aster and Skare. But she had it now, and what good was knowledge if it was never put to use? She hiked for the better part of an hour out to a stand of exposed rock jutting up from a favorite grazing pasture for the herd. In the darkest parts of winter, when sunlight could be measured in moments and the dead remains of the last season's grass crunched underfoot, wild reindeer could still graze on the lichen that grew on the stones and glean enough nutrition to carry them through. Fortunately for her, there was still ample grass for the roaming herds. Gerda scraped a large patch of the lichen from the stone face into a sample jar she carried in her bag, and resealed the lid when she was satisfied that she had enough. She hoped it wouldn't be too late by the time she arrived back in the village.

Skare was waiting for her when Gerda returned to the cabin for the book with the cure. "You're leaving," the queen said from the door as Gerda tucked the tome against the jar in her bag.

"Yes," Gerda confirmed, trying not to meet the other woman's gaze. She didn't know yet what she would find there. "I - I have to go back to my village. I can help them, but I have to go now or it might be too late."

"They were cruel to you," Skare said flatly.

"They were," Gerda agreed, finally looking at the woman in the doorway. "When they were children. And now, they need help. Their children need my help. Maybe they won't be any better as adults, but I can help them with everything that I've learned here. You came here when you found your calling. Now, I think that I've found mine."

"They do not deserve you, child," the queen

said more softly, her icy eyes softening as much as Gerda had ever seen.

"Maybe, but I'm still going. And if I don't want to stay, I won't. I'll come back."

"The roses will need tending," Skare replied, her voice cracking softly like footsteps on packsnow. Gerda felt tears prickling at the corners of her eyes. The queen stepped forward and brushed the escaping moisture away from her bare cheeks. "No tears. They will freeze, and you will be back."

Gerda nodded, then stepped in for an embrace. The queen's arms wrapped around her, the embrace cold and warm all at once. When she stepped back, she found she wore a leather satchel on her back. It's weight was substantial, but not more than she could carry on her journey. "Thank you. Mother."

"Take the sledge. The reindeer know the way, and the way back home." Skare released her.

"Thank you," Gerda said again, adjusting the new bag on her shoulder, and started for the door.

The First Snow

Jill Cronbaugh

"Promise me." She takes off her fuzzy pink mitten and holds out a stiffened pinky. He pulls off his dino glove and solemnly wraps his pinky around hers. Tears shine in his eyes as hers slowly run down her cheeks. He touches his reddened nose to her cold, slightly damp nose tip.

"Every year. No matter what," he says.

"Son! The truck's leaving NOW! Let's GO!"

The snow lightly falls on her lavender knit pompom hat as she watches the moving truck take him away.

. . . .

The majordomo tightens his thin lips in disapproval as she stomps her heel into the stylish fur-lined boots.

"Miss. A young lady of fifteen does NOT galavant through the town to meet a boy!"

She pats his cheek with her bemittened hand.

"He has not failed to meet me for the first snow in six years." She smiles gently into his concerned eyes. "You know what this means to me. I'll be back by the end of the day. No following me. I will know."

Iowa [W]rites of Winter

Her gleaming pink vespa weaves through the traffic. Fewer and fewer cars impede her progress the closer she gets to the small neighborhood park's bridge. The weather radar was definitive. Today is the day for snow.

She slows to a crawling pace as she maneuvers the narrow trails of the park, passing elders on the few benches gazing at the river, children speeding, screeching to the playground, and one couple, of indeterminate age, holding hands while walking toward the center gazebo. The first tiny snowflakes fall as she nears the ornate little bridge.

She parks the vespa at the foot of the bridge, takes a deep breath, and slowly climbs the stairs to the bridge proper. He's beaten her there four of the last six years. She is thrilled, and slightly annoyed, to see he's beaten her again. His face lights up as she walks toward him.

"How do you get here before me?!"

He wraps his arms around her and squeezes tight enough for her to feel his muscular, lanky arms through his puffy winter coat. She laughs and kisses his cheek as he releases her. The snowflakes grow to a more respectable size and dance in the breeze. They watch the beautiful scene hand in hand until she shivers involuntarily.

"Do you really want to know?"

His eyes twinkle as she nods. He takes her hand and leads her off the bridge to the small forested area at the edge of the park. There, just inside the stand of trees, is a dark green tent. It's just wide enough for four people to lie side by side. He takes in her shocked silence and chuckles.

The First Snow

"I've come three times this winter. Weather forecasters are so unreliable."

They brush the accumulated snow off each other's heads and shoulders, then he takes her hands and steers her through the entryway butt-first. She plops on the ground, and he pulls off her boots so she can scoot into the tent. He then follows. The floor of the tent is cushioned by layers of blankets atop unrolled yoga mats. Cocooned in blankets, they cuddle and watch the snow in silence. Dusk creeps along the edges of the sky and she sighs. She strokes his hair and presses her cold cheek to his. His mouth curves as he takes off his gloves and gently places his warm hands on either side of her face. She closes her eyes and presses her lips to his. Time stops.

. . . .

She tightens the belt of her wool duster and grabs her earmuffs from her desk. Quickly striding in her sensible, yet stylish boots, she tries to make it past her secretary.

"Ma'am! You've got four meetings this afternoon!"

Her joyful smile stops the predictable nagging.

"Reschedule them. I'll be back tomorrow."

She nearly skips out the door. Looking up at the sky, she curses under her breath as the valet takes an eternity to retrieve her car. After nearly twenty years, she isn't going to be late now! She wills the weather to stay with her as she nears the old neighborhood park. Wishing she still had her vespa so she could get closer to the bridge, she runs down the now-paved pathways to the renovated bridge. Taking the steps two at a time, she makes it to the top as the snow starts to fall. She leans on the rail to catch her breath as he laughs at her entrance. He walks over to her. She kicks the side of his shoe and laughs with him.

He pulls her into his side, and she puts her arm around his waist. Still chuckling, he kisses her cheek with his cold lips.

"You didn't have to run so hard. I'll always be here."

She flexes her arm to hold him even tighter.

"It's special this year." She reaches her leather-gloved hand into her pocket and gives him a small square of thin paper. "I've been saving this for two weeks. I was hoping it would snow soon. I couldn't have waited much longer."

He stares at the ultrasound for a few stunned moments then whoops and swings her around and around in his arms. They laugh and kiss as the snow coats their hair and eyelashes.

. . . .

She pokes her head into the livingroom. Her children, home for winter break, look up from the tv, laptops, and phones.

"I need you all to finish making supper."
None of them move. "NOW!"

She slides into the hall in her fuzzy socks and throws on her sensible boots. As she pulls on her pink parka, her oldest whines.

The First Snow

"You're still doing this? C'mon!"

She laughs over her shoulder at her offspring as she runs out the door.

"In 45 years, I've never been late. I'm not starting now! Don't burn the house down."

She hops out of the cab and jogs carefully through the slick, misty wet snow to the in-need-of-renovation bridge. She hears a reedy whistle as she nears the steps and grins. It's their song, but very flat. She softly sings as she crests the top of the stairs. His face lights up at the sight of her. He swings her around in his arms and gently sets her on her feet next to him.

"It's my turn for a surprise." He grins hard as his eyes smile in triumph. "We don't have to worry about them tearing down the bridge."

Open mouthed, she stares at him with delight. "What happened?"

He presents her with a stack of papers. "We bought the park. Happy anniversary!"

Tears cascade down her cheeks. He smiles gently until she grabs him and pulls his head down to hers to kiss him senseless.

. . . .

She swiftly zips her three-year-old's jacket and completes bundling her infant as she cajoles her ten-year-old into his winter gear.

"C'mon! Please hurry! It's going to start snowing any minute now!"

"We gonna go play in the snow, Mommy? Where we goin'?"

Her ten-year-old grabs his sister's hand and pulls her to the mini-van.

She tenderly bounces the baby to keep him from fussing as she climbs the stairs to the new bench on the bridge. Her children sit next to her in silence, the three-year-old clutching her big brother's hand. He smiles down at her in approval and she beams.

As the snow starts to gently fall, a male and female cardinal land on the bridge rail. They flutter-hop next to each other and sit in silence. The male gives a tiny shake of his tail and chirps a flat tune. He turns to the female to preen her feathers.

She slowly turns the baby in her arms so he can see the birds. She kisses the top of his little hooded head and strokes her other children's' bobble-hatted heads.

"Grandma and Grandpa never miss the first snow of the year."

The Last Kiss of Winter

Dennis Maulsby

Ticker tapes of snow spin
down in ribbons and bows.

Wind knits spring grass
into green and white afghans,

crochets lace doilies over
the winking dragon eyes

of ruby, gold, and emerald
dangling above intersections.

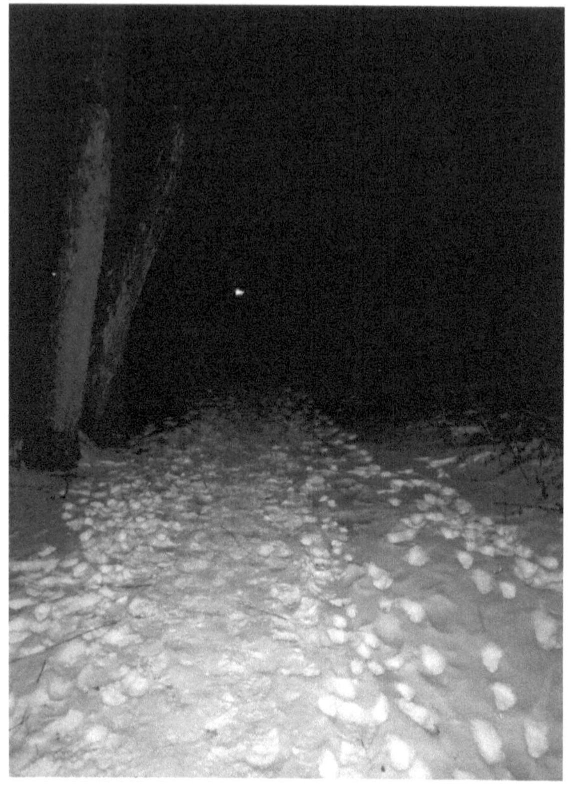

Christmas Night

Spike Dawkins

Winter haiku chain

Dennis Maulsby

flakes pile up thick dunes
winds sculpt bleached topiary
fur-faced mice tunnel

crows forage in fields
squawk, shake wings over spilled corn
black dancers on snow

in the birthing dawn
a gray coyote dog-trots
raising puffs of snow

above winter haze
an owl rides on a whisper
wings dip in and out

Chilled

Rachel Schneberger

She saw a squirrel die today,
fell from a tree
onto the snowy ground
its icy touch, paralyzing.
She could notice it squirming
trying to move it's broken body
but the movements slowed, idling.
She watches the scene
from the window, unsure,
filled with innate aid.
But how?
Out the door
marching toward,
uncomfortable that it doesn't
scurry away.
The squirrel, alive,
a slow breath,
a wide gash across its head,
and the ruby red of blood
stains dripping onto white.
She gently scoops it up
recognizing her incapacity to rescue,
intent to offer solace.
Yet she's standing knee deep in snow,
crying, pondering,
how to tenderly accompany this creature
in its final ceasing.
She lay the squirrel,
still breathing,
back upon the snow
in a spot with lots of sun.
A final bath, a blessing,
in a warm glow.

Chilled

Returning inside, remorseful,
steadfastly keeps her gaze
out the window
with a view of the stationary squirrel,
hoping to see it move again
mostly wondering
how it feels to freeze to death.

Winter's Prey

Erin Casey

Viola Farkas nestled deep into a colorful, granny-square afghan to stave off the winter chill. A fire crackled merrily in the stone fireplace beside her aspen log chair. She propped her slippered feet on the ottoman in front of her and tilted her head back, enjoying the blessed quiet. It was nice to get away from the city, especially after her most recent assignment. The noise got to her and left her craving the comfort of her family's cabin. These days, few people visited, leaving the cabin's care in Viola's hands. She poured her love into it, replacing old, decayed logs and updating the inside to provide more modern comforts like a gas stove and indoor plumbing.

I'm glad I installed new windows before the winter storm came in, she thought, glancing at the three windows adjacent to a reading nook. Snow fell in fat flakes, and icicles nearly the length of her forearm clung to the roof. The very sight made Viola shiver and duck her head further into her blanket.

At least until a loud whistle blew in the kitchen.

Vi groaned. Just when she was getting comfortable, too! She dragged herself from her blanket cocoon and shuffled into the kitchen. The tea kettle continued screeching until Vi turned off the stove. She poured boiling water into a mug that read, "Books Are My Happy Place" in big bold letters. An English Breakfast tea bag floated to the top of the mug. Vi breathed it in and held it between her chilly hands.

"Hmm, much better," she murmured to herself and walked into the living room.

A figure sitting in the reading nook nearly made her jump out of her skin.

"Josie!" Vi exclaimed. She grabbed the wall to steady herself. "Jesus, you have to stop scaring me like that."

Josie kept her attention on the window, a red blanket draped around her shoulders and head. "The wolves are out hunting."

Vi paused. She glanced at the glass then back at Josie. Her shoulders slumped. "We're at the cabin. Of course wolves will be out chasing something." She returned to her chair and almost sat down, but her sister's lack of response made her sigh. She draped the afghan over her arm and dragged it, and herself, over to the reading nook. "Did you see them?"

Josie shook her head and looked over at Vi. Her pretty golden hair flowed around her face, her brown eyes dancing with firelight. "No, but I can hear them," she said.

Vi pursed her lips. Reluctantly, she grasped the bottom of the central window and cracked it open. Icy wind spilled into the cabin, causing Vi to shiver. As she listened, she made out a faint howl. "Wolves hunt all the time. It doesn't have to be something nefarious."

"Keep listening," Josie said.

Vi closed her eyes, praying for patience, and waited.

A scream pierced the air. The taunting howl in response told her this wasn't a normal hunt.

Werewolf.

So much for a peaceful night.

"Shit," she growled to herself. She slammed the window shut and locked it, fighting the urge to stay wrapped up in her warm blankets, clasping her hot tea. Josie stared at her, waiting. "I can't solve everyone's problems."

"Vi…"

With another curse, Vi threw her blanket off and banged her mug down so hard, the ceramic cracked. Vi ignored it and stormed over to a wardrobe with a keypad deadbolt. She tapped in the number and opened the doors. Behind it was a personal arsenal.

She searched through the weapons and grabbed two Colt Python revolvers with silver bullets, a crossbow with silver-tipped bolts, and two daggers. She strapped the weapons around her waist and right thigh and set the crossbow on a table while she pulled on a long grayish white coat that would camouflage her in the snow. Similarly-colored gloves covered her hands, and she tied a mask around her mouth to limit breathing in the revolver's smokey discharge.

After belting her coat and strapping the crossbow to her arm, she slid into her combat boots.

Josie hurried to her side, a red cloak replacing the blanket. "Ready."

"Stay here," Vi said and gave her sister a fierce look. "I can handle this."

"You know you can't make me stay. I'm coming whether you like it or not."

Vi curled her lip, not that Josie could see it behind her mask, then snorted. "Fine," she muttered. "Let's make this quick." She yanked open the door and waited for Josie to go out first before she followed and locked the cabin behind her.

All I wanted was one quiet night, damn it, she thought bitterly as she trekked through the snow. Yak tracks on her boots prevented her from sliding on patches of ice, and the howling wind drowned out the sound of her steps, mostly. The howls and screams were far louder anyway. She doubted anyone would notice her approach, except by smell.

Josie kept up with her. "You could go faster if you—"

"I'm *not* doing that unless I have to," Vi replied curtly. She glanced at her sister and instantly regretted her tone. Josie was just trying to help, and bless her, she only wanted to protect innocent people. But Vi was *tired*.

It seemed like more and more werewolves showed up where they weren't wanted. If they just behaved, kept to their packs, then it wouldn't be a problem. But many of them craved violence and took it out on folks who didn't deserve it. A bite didn't always transform a person; more often, it killed. Not everybody was compatible with werewolf venom. Vi had ended more than a few bite victims just to put them out of their misery.

From the sound of the screams, she had a feeling she'd be digging a couple of fresh graves tonight.

The ground dipped down, and Vi maneuvered her way to the bottom. She crouched behind the snowy underbrush and cautiously looked over the top. At first, it was hard to see the fight in the swirl of wind and snow. White flakes nested on her eyelashes, causing her to blink repeatedly.

Suddenly, a hulking brown figure darted in front of her and threw a young boy, a teenager by Vi's guess, into the snow. He was dressed in his PJs, though one sleeve was missing, and the right side of his shorts was drenched in blood.

"Evan!" a girl screamed as she collapsed beside him. She shook in her torn spaghetti-strap nightshirt and fluffy pink pants. She yanked him away as a huge white werewolf rose up in front of them.

On two feet, the werewolf was nearly 8-feet tall. He walked on digitigrade legs, with most of his weight resting on his toes. His broad head tapered to a narrow muzzle filled with bloody, gnashing teeth. He grinned at the two trembling teens while the other two werewolves, one brown, one gray, pincered them in.

"Please! Don't hurt us!" the girl sobbed. Snot and tears ran down her face while she tried to keep the wounded boy behind her. "J-just let us go!"

The wolves released sounds that reminded Vi of hyena cackles. She gritted her teeth and pulled out her revolvers. As the white alpha raised his paws to pounce on the sobbing girl, Vi opened fire. Silver bullets cut through the air, taking the brown wolf through the head, and clipping the black one on her hip. The alpha dropped low, a bullet taking off his ear, but otherwise he remained unscathed. He looked over at the dead brown werewolf and howled in rage.

"You missed him," Josie scolded. "He was like five feet in front of you!"

Vi fired another shot as the white werewolf turned toward the bush, likely smelling the smoke. He dodged and pounced.

Vi threw herself to the ground, rolling as he sailed past her. She heard the black wolf whimpering over the brown until the alpha snarled at it. Suddenly the black wolf joined him, and Vi heard two more answering howls.

Shit! Of *course* there would be more. Three would be too easy!

Vi scrambled to her feet, reloading her two revolvers, one at a time. "Come and get me!" she shouted. If she drew them away from the kids, they might stand a chance. The wolves followed close behind, the snow hardly impeding them. Vi whipped around a tree, turned, and fired. The black wolf went down with bullets in her front leg and chest, but the alpha still managed to evade her attacks.

He looked back, and Vi followed his gaze.

The black wolf slowly shrank. Fur sucked back into her body, while her legs crunched and rippled, taking on human ones instead. A naked woman, gasping for breath, lay in the snow, her eyes rolled up toward the sky. Blood flowed from her wounds where black-like lines spiderwebbed out from the gaping holes. She rolled her head toward the alpha. With a weak smile, a final white plume left her lips, and she went still.

The alpha whined and whipped his head around toward Vi. The murderous gleam in his eyes sent her running again, though not without firing another shot at him. He dodged and raced after her.

As Vi ran, the cold bit her face. The snow grew deeper, dragging her legs down like quicksand. This wasn't working! Any moment the other wolves would appear, if the alpha didn't kill her first!

I have to do it. If I don't, I'll die, and so will the kids.

Her leg sank again, and she pitched forward at the same time the alpha tried to pounce her. He landed inches in front of her and spun. Vi lifted her guns, only to have them smacked out of her hands. His sharp claws tore into her jacket as he grabbed her by the front and yanked her out of the snow. Vi pulled her dagger free and sliced his arm. He yowled, dropping her.

Vi drove her dagger into his gut with as much force as she could muster. The alpha screamed in pain.

Something slammed into her so hard, she was sent flying through the icy air. She hit the ground, rolling, until her back struck a tree. Her weapons were scattered around her. She lay on her side and watched as another white wolf helped yank the dagger out of the alpha's stomach. He coughed and leaned against the female for support. The new wolf was bigger than the alpha!

Unless…unless *this* was the other alpha, his mate.

"Get up, Vi! Get up!" Josie yelled at her from behind the tree. "Don't just lie there."

Vi groaned and struggled to sit up as the she-wolf laid the male down into the snow to recover. Another gray wolf loped out of the woods and bared his teeth at Vi. With a nod from the alphess, the gray howled and rushed Vi.

Vi yanked off her coat and spread her hands.

Silver fur rippled over her body as it grew from a tiny human to a giant, powerful werewolf. Her mouth morphed into a vicious maw, her legs rearranging until her toes dug into the snow. Her hands quadrupled in size with razor sharp claws. With a snarl, she caught the gray wolf by his paws and yanked him forward. She sank her teeth into his neck and shook her head savagely until his body went still.

Vi dropped him to the ground at the same time the alphess barreled into her. They sank into the snow, claws slashing, teeth digging into paw, arm, and shoulder. Vi yelped in pain as fangs ripped a chunk of meat from her bicep. Ruby blood stained the pristine snow, leaving a trail that ended with Vi on the bottom, and the white wolf on top. Vi snarled, her paws clinging to the wolf's throat as she tried to keep the alphess's face away from her neck.

"*Traitor!*" the werewolf roared at her in a sound only other werewolves would understand.

"*I'm not letting you kill them,*" Vi growled back. "*They're under my protection.*"

The wolf snapped her teeth near Vi's face. "*They kill us for sport. We're just returning the favor. Cull the young before they can pick up a gun, like you. You're one of us! Why kill us?"*

Vi's eyes burned with rage. She clawed the werewolf's chest. *"No I'm not. I'm this thing because of deranged werewolves like you! Your people are the reason my family is dead! And I swear I'll hunt down every one of you so long as you're a threat to humans."*

The werewolf roared again and drove her claws into Vi's sides. Vi howled and started to lose her grip on the female's mouth.

"Vi! Fight back!" Josie screamed at her.

Vi closed her eyes and drove her foot into the wolf's stomach, claws digging for purchase. It distracted the alphess long enough for Vi to lunge forward and rip her throat out with her fangs. The werewolf gasped and collapsed on top of Vi, her dead body shifting back to human, leaving a naked woman on Vi's chest. Vi flopped her head in the snow with a groan. Her body *hurt*. She didn't transform often, which made things ache anyway, and the bites on her shoulder and claw marks on her side didn't help.

She pushed the woman off of her and climbed carefully to her paws.

Her ears perked suddenly to the familiar click of her gun. Vi looked up.

The teenage girl stood trembling in the snow, her hands wrapped around the revolver. Her teeth chattered, frozen tears glistening on her cheeks. She kept the gun trained. "D-don't move!" she stuttered

Vi looked down at the dead woman at her feet. Shit. This looked bad. Of course, now she looked like the villain, and she couldn't communicate in this form; only other werewolves would understand her growls. By the time she transformed back, the girl would have shot her. Vi huffed out a breath and lifted her paws in a peaceful gesture.

The girl frowned in confusion. She started to lower the gun.

Vi nodded.

Something snarled nearby. Vi barely had time to look before the first alpha, who she'd completely forgotten about in the snow, leapt at the teenager. The girl screamed and fired. The bullet ripped through his shoulder, but he knocked her to the ground, causing the gun to fly free.

"*No!*" Vi roared and threw herself at the wolf, knowing she'd be too late.

Josie appeared behind the alpha and grabbed his tail in her small hands. She yanked as hard as she could. The wolf staggered, his jaws just missing the frightened girl's face.

Vi snatched him around the head. Without mercy, she twisted as hard as she could. His neck snapped with a loud crunch. She tossed his limp body to the ground. Vi panted, holding her side. She looked at the teenager, expecting to find her mangled. But the girl stared up at her with wide, panicked eyes, her lips turning blue from the cold. Vi took her in, noting her cut and bloody feet. How long had the wolves chased the kids?

Vi whined in her throat, making herself sound far more like a dog than a vicious werewolf. The kid needed warmth before anything else. Who knew if the other one was still alive? She reached down and pulled the girl to her. Exhaustion kept the teen from struggling. Vi held her, letting the warmth of her body and fur breathe life into her freezing form. The girl shivered after a while, a good sign all things considered. Vi felt her tuck her feet against Vi's body, adding more blood to her fur, but she didn't mind.

Vi nuzzled the teen and looked over at Josie. Her sister stood over the male alpha's body, staring at her hands. She opened and closed them.

Vi sent her a questioning woof, drawing Josie's attention. Her sister shook herself. "I'll go check on the other one."

Before Vi could argue, her sister fled into the white wall of snow.

Vi lingered with the teenager for a short while, resting. She usually relied on her weapons to fight werewolves, not her claws. Had she been on an actual hunt, she would have been more prepared, but the cabin provided only a small supply of weapons. She'd live to fight another day, both as a human and as a werewolf.

The teenager stirred. "I need to help my brother."

Vi looked down at her and nodded. She shifted her grip on the teen and got her up onto Vi's back so she could ride. It would be warmer that way. Vi padded over to her fallen gun and gestured to it with her nose. The teen leaned down and picked it up, then the second gun when Vi found it.

She wasn't going to leave those behind. The rest she could pick up later, but guns specially made for silver bullets were hard to come by.

The last thing they recovered was Vi's jacket so the girl wouldn't die of cold.

Vi loped back to the clearing, the teen gripping her fur tightly so she wouldn't fall off. She followed the blood trail and nosed through the bushes.

Josie knelt next to the teen. He didn't move or shiver. Vi thought they were too late, until her sensitive ears picked up a weak heartbeat. The girl tried to hop down, but Vi growled at her in warning and reached for the boy instead. Carefully, she lifted him up and passed him off to his sister. Between her fur and the jacket, at least the pair would stay warm.

Vi ran as quickly as she dared back to the cabin. She was grateful for the falling snow which would cover her tracks in case anyone came upon the scene before she could dispose of the bodies. Not to mention she didn't need any stragglers following her home.

Once they reached the cabin, Vi nosed at her coat until the teen reached in and pulled out a key. She slid off Vi's back, unlocked the door, and pushed it open. Vi nudged her inside with her nose and turned sideways. The teen pulled her brother off Vi's back and stepped away from the door. The frame was too small for Vi's massive form.

Grunting, Vi transformed back into a human on her doorstep. Her skin prickled with the cold the moment her fur disappeared. She held out a partially formed arm to the teen, gesturing to her coat. When the girl passed it over, Vi wrapped it around herself, hiding her naked body. She really didn't care, but she figured the teens didn't need to see it. Vi shook her hair out a little and stepped inside once she was fully formed.

"All right, let's get you two cleaned up. I'm Viola, but you can just call me Vi. What's your name, kid?"

"I'm Kari," the teen replied quietly.

Fortunately, Kari didn't waste time with questions. She was so worried about her brother, she let a werewolf take him from her arms and carry him toward the living room fire. "Grab those blankets and pillows and get them set up on the ground. Keep a couple for yourself."

Kari did as ordered and had a makeshift bed set up before long. Vi laid him on top of the blankets and started to inspect him. Cuts and bruises decorated his body, but those didn't matter to her. No, the gaping wound on his leg was the bigger concern. She used warm water and soap to wipe away the blood until she saw the source of the wound.

Vi's shoulders fell. The kid had been bitten. Which would explain the fever suddenly running through his body. She sighed. It was too late to amputate his leg. The bite was fresh, yes, but the fever indicated the venom was already invading his system.

"Were you bitten?" Vi asked the girl.

Kari clasped her brother's hand in hers as she huddled beneath a blanket. "No. They tried, but they missed." Tears pricked her eyes. "I tried to protect him. I didn't…I didn't mean—"

"Shh," Vi said in a quieter tone. "It's not your fault. Those wolves were ready to either turn or kill you. The fact you're both alive proves how strong you are." She shook her head and ran her fingers through her hair. "I need to get some supplies. Stay with him."

Vi went to her bedroom and threw off her coat. She climbed into her shower to rinse off so her blood didn't get all over the teens while she tended to them. Her wounds had mostly healed over, but she spent a few minutes bandaging herself. She pulled on fresh clothes and grabbed baggy pants and shirts for both teens. She turned toward the hallway and found Josie standing in front of the door.

"I'm sorry I couldn't help more," Josie said quietly. She held her red blanket close.

"You did plenty," Vi reassured her. "More than I expected." She smiled sadly at her sister and returned to the teens.

Vi worked in silence, bandaging up the boy first and making sure he was dressed and comfortable before she helped the girl. She offered a shower to her, but Kari shook her head and changed into the new clothes instead.

"I don't want to leave his side." She sat down by him and stroked his hair.

Vi heated up a few cups of hot chocolate, using the microwave this time. She added protein powder to both, figuring Kari could use a boost after being stuck out in the snow like that.

She passed one over to her and sat down heavily in her log chair. "That's the best we can do for him. Now we wait."

"To see if the bite kills him or turns him into a werewolf," Kari said bluntly.

Vi lifted an eyebrow. "You know about us then?"

Kari nodded, looking into her swirling hot chocolate as she gripped the mug for warmth. "Yeah. Our aunt told us stories. She talked about werewolves and the people who hunted them. She was a hunter too." Her eyes watered. "After our parents died, our aunt took us in. She brought us out here for winter break to give us time to be together as a family. She said, once we were old enough, she'd teach us about hunting. But then those monsters barged in, killed her, and chased us out into the snow." She blinked and glanced sideways at Vi. "No offense."

Vi shrugged. "I've been called worse. Do you know why they attacked you?"

Kari shook her head. "Before they chased us out the door, I saw two of them devouring my aunt. Evan and I didn't even have a chance to put our boots on. We just ran. And they chased us until you appeared." She brushed her brother's hair again. "I don't get it. You're one of them. Why did you help us?"

"I'm not like them," Vi said with a growl then caught herself when Kari flinched. She wrinkled her nose. The kid didn't know any better. She set her drink down and leaned forward, arms draped over her legs. "Look, I'm kind of like your brother. My family and I were attacked too, a long, *long,* time ago. Parents were killed. My sister and I were both bitten." She glanced over at Josie as her sister sat down in the reading nook. "I survived the transformation. Hated what I'd become. A hunter caught me when I was in hiding. Taught me how to hunt my own kind and said I had an advantage because I could transform. I could withstand more damage and smell or hear them out. So, I decided, if I was going to be this thing, I'd use my new skills for good."

"Do you kill *all* werewolves?" Kari asked cautiously, her hand stilling on her brother's head.

"No, just the ones who cause problems. Lot of werewolves live peacefully. They go about their business, don't bug anyone." She flexed her fingers. "I go after the ones who hurt people. Like the ones that killed your aunt. Being a werewolf for me is both a gift and a curse." Some days she wished she'd died with the rest of her family. And others, well, she was glad she could make a difference and save people.

Kari bowed her head and fought back tears, but they flowed anyway. "My aunt always told us to fear them. Evan's going to think he's a monster if he survives."

Vi pursed her lips, leaning back. "He's only a monster if he makes himself one. He's still your brother. And he can live an honest, safe, and happy life. But not alone. He needs a pack, whether that's other werewolves or you, he just can't be alone."

Kari rubbed her eyes. "What can I do?"

"You love him, cherish him, remind him he's not a burden, no matter what form he's in." Vi glanced over at Josie. Her sister smiled back, the falling snow through the window framing her beautifully. "And you have patience with him as he learns his new body."

"I...I don't know a lot about werewolves, just what my aunt told me. But I won't stop loving him. He's my little brother. I'm not going anywhere."

Vi stared at the pair. For a moment, she imagined herself and Josie, her on the ground with Josie kneeling beside.

If only they'd been so lucky.

Vi sighed. "Do you and Evan have any family left?"

Kari shook her head as more tears rolled down her cheeks. "No. Our aunt was the last member of our family. I don't know what we're going to do. I'm not 18 yet, so we'll get thrown into the system and—"

"Slow down," Vi said as Kari started getting worked up. "I know folks who can take you both in. They've housed humans and werewolves. Until then, you can stay with me, and I'll teach him about being a werewolf, and help you understand what you can do to help him. Sound good?"

"Why-why would you do that?"

"Like I said, I figure if I'm forced to be a werewolf, I'll use it for whatever good I can. I'll still have to go on missions and such, but I'm not usually gone long, and I'll keep home stacked with food." Vi stood up and rolled her shoulders. "Think about it. And get some rest. He'll be out for a while." If he ever woke again.

Vi set her drink down and headed for the door.

"Where are you going?" Kari asked anxiously.

"To take care of the bodies. We don't need anyone coming across them and either wanting revenge, or bringing the police out here. It's better if we're not found." Especially if she had to train a new werewolf. "I won't be gone long. Rest."

Vi pulled another coat on and slipped into a fresh pair of boots. She grabbed a shovel from the weapons cabinet, but instead of going out the front, she went out back to the garden her family had planted years ago.

It served another purpose these days.

"That was really sweet, what you said," Josie murmured as she appeared beside Vi. "About how she should love him and remind him he's not a burden."

"I meant every word," Viola replied and glanced at her sister. She stopped before one of the grave stones nestled beneath the bare branches of a willow tree. Vi crouched and brushed the snow off of it, gazing at the name written across its surface.

Josephine Farkas.

Vi hung her head. "I know I act annoyed when you show up to help me. It's not because I'm not happy to see you. I just…"

Josie placed a hand on her shoulder that she couldn't feel. "You still blame yourself."

"I should have protected you," Vi said, fighting the old pain scarring her heart. "Why did I survive the change, but you didn't?"

Josie shrugged her shoulders. "None of what happened was your fault, Viola. And I'll remind you of that each and every time I find you."

Vi shut her eyes against the tears threatening to fall. "I wish you could rest and be at peace."

"One day. But for now, I'll gladly help my big sister." Josie wrapped her arms around Vi in a ghostly hug. Vi returned it and mimicked patting her arm. "For now, I need to rest and restore my essence."

"You pushed yourself too much today," Vi scolded gently. It was rare for Josie to make herself corporeal, but she'd done it to stop the wolf. To save Vi and the girl.

Vi cleaned the grave off some more and looked up at her little sister. "Sleep well, Josie. I love you."

"I love you, too." With a smile, Josie floated over to her grave in her little red blanket and sank into her snowy bed.

It had snowed that day too, the last time Vi saw her sister's living smile. She remembered Josie dancing in the falling flakes, laughing as they turned her cheeks red. Hours later, two bites took Josie from her and cursed Vi. They were left writhing in agony on the ground while the snow blanketed them, threatening to devour them like they were winter's prey.

Vi shook her head and rose. She stepped out into the swirling white forest, the shovel clutched tightly in her hand. She had work to do.

Species Shift

Dennis Maulsby

I slow-step through chill skim milk fog, arms out,
booted feet tender on ice-glazed grass.

The forest surrounds me. Branches crusted thick
with frozen fog whiskers, half snow, half lace,
change into coral heads, reefs. Misty currents

eddy, blend into swirling ocean banners.
My lungs fill and empty, transform the ordinary,
spout liquid threads high into the haze.

Sounds come in humid pulses, ratcheting
clicks, high-pitched whistles and moans,
whale songs casting spells of salt and seaweed.

I sense the passage of schools of glittering scales.
From my flesh tail and fins bud, grow, push.
My body flexes in muscled ripples, knife-slices

through cold buoyant vapor.
Skin satin black and cream, I am Orca,
rows of finger-long conical teeth, smiling.

Contributors

Contributors

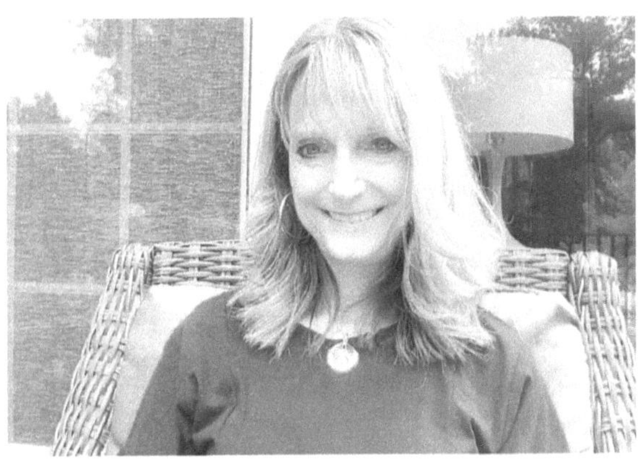

Judith F. Brenner (she/her), a Chicago native, wrote *The Moments Between Dreams, a Novel,* (Greenleaf Book Press, 2022) which won four fiction awards in the US and one in the UK. She owns Creative Lakes Media, LLC, and completed the Iowa University Summer Writing Mini-MFA in 2019. Author website: JudithFBrenner.com

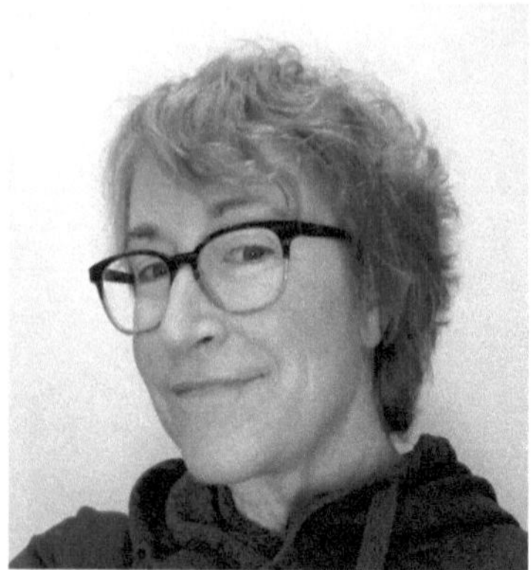

Kelli Brommel (she/her) is a writer, a librarian,
and a former teacher. She lives with her partner
and zero pets in Iowa City. Her nest isn't so much
empty as it is filled with her kids' stuff.

Contributors

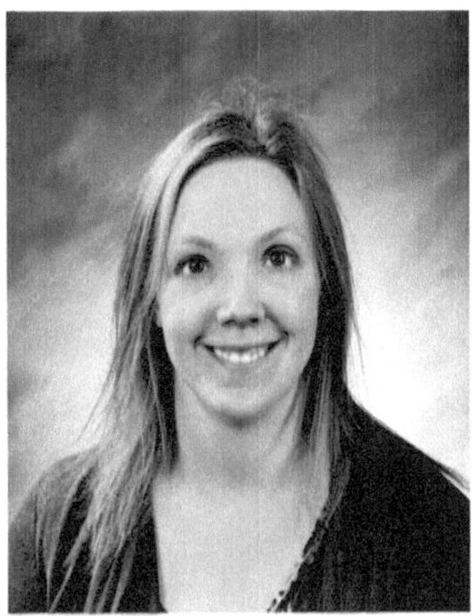

JE Brooke (she/her) is an anthropologist by day, science fiction and fantasy writer by night. When she isn't writing stories and novels, she can be found knitting or cross-stitching nerdy things, or lost in the pages of a good book. She can be found on Instagram as je_brooke_thewriter

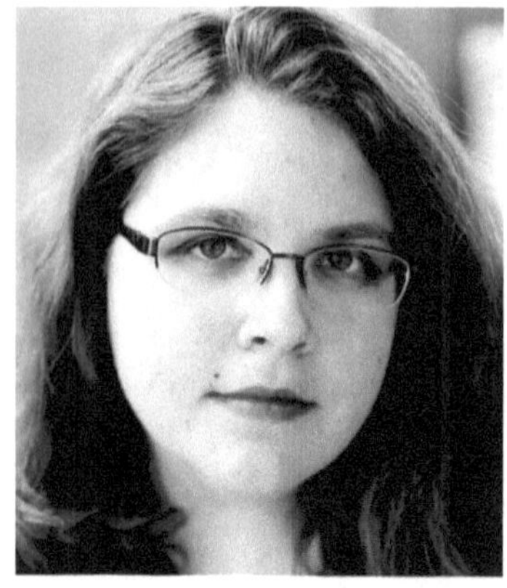

Erin Casey (she/her) is an urban fantasy writer and author of The Purple Door District series. The first completed trilogy follows the stories of parahumans (werebirds, vampires, werewolves, fae, witches, magi, etc.) living in safe havens called Purple Door Districts. Learn more at erincasey. org.

Contributors

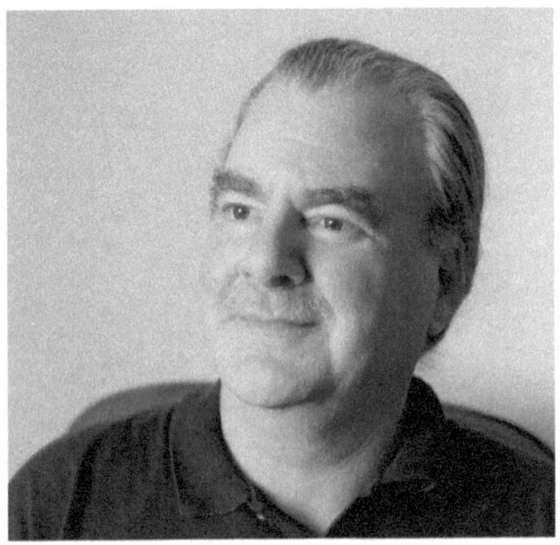

G.Z. Chapman (he/him) often wonders how ancient soot marks made eons ago on cave walls has led to all this.

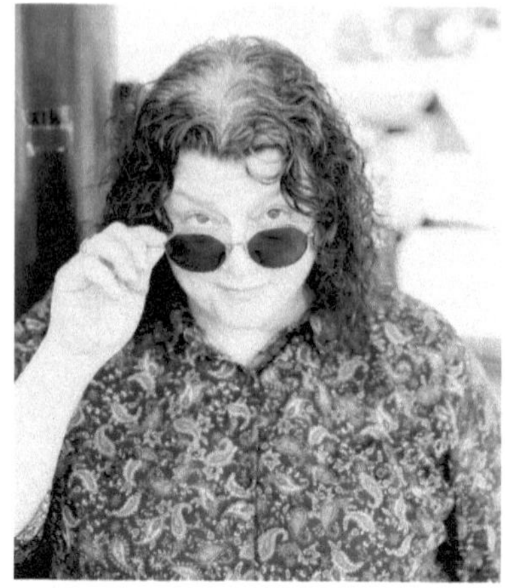

Jill Cronbaugh (she/her) hates writing author bios. Her first piece was a short-story at the age of 6 about the time her grandpa took her to steal some field corn for her pony. The reviews were great! It delighted her grandfather and embarrassed her mother — all-in-all, a job well done!

Contributors

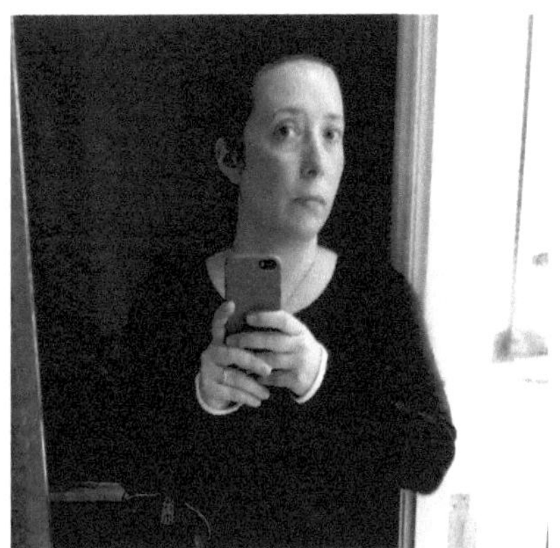

Spike Dawkins (she/her) is the pen name of a photographer and writer of horror and crime fiction. Her novel in progress, Lost Boys, was shortlisted for the Crime Writers' Association Debut Dagger Award in 2017. She lives in Iowa City.

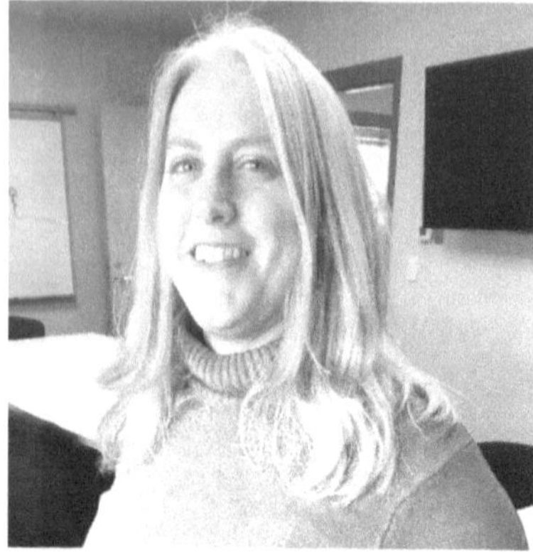

Sharon Falduto (she/her) works at Kirkwood, helping International and English language learner students. She is an avid reader and volunteers with the Iowa Radio Reading Network. She lives in Coralville with her husband and three daughters.

Contributors

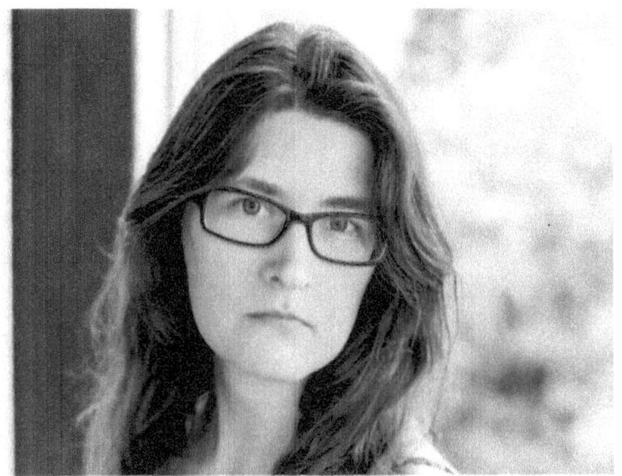

Amy Ford (she/her) works as an associate photographer for CTW Photography. She lives in North Liberty, IA with her family.

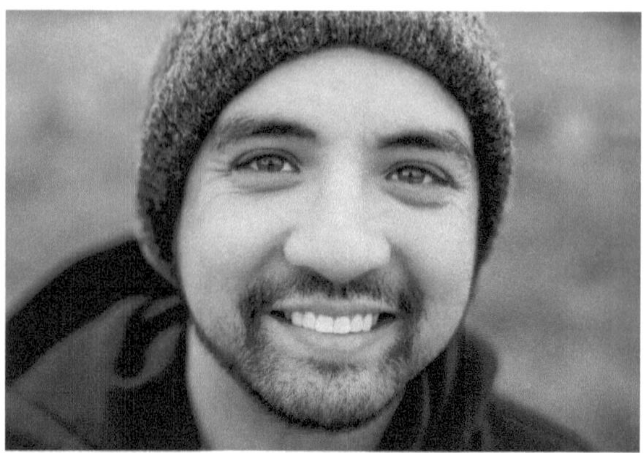

William Ford (he/him) is an amateur photographer trying to live his best life in North Liberty with his family and two cats.

Contributors

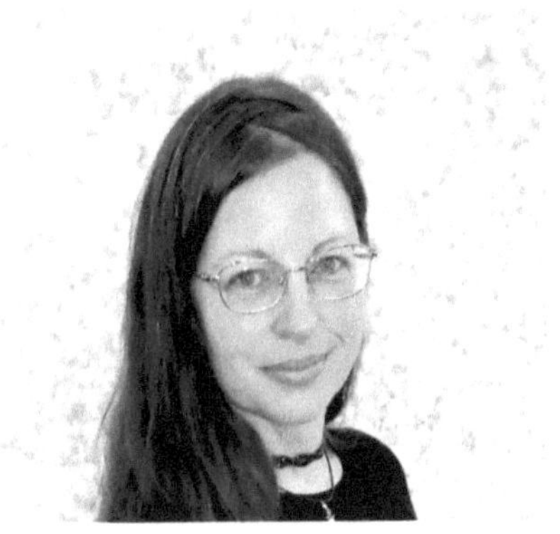

Sharon Ruth Hensley (she/her) Fond of truth, justice, and folks staying out of each other's way, Sharon Ruth Hensley is a multi-genre writer who has been primarily poeting since the eighties.

Winter is her favorite season. She possesses a deep appreciation for the peace and power present in Iowa snowfall.

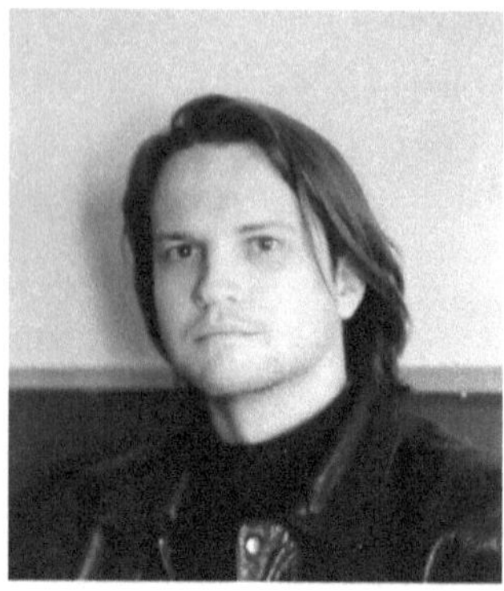

Malcolm MacDougall (he/they) is a writer and a poet who draws on his experience as a queer man growing up in Catholic Midwestern culture. He has been published in Fools Magazine, Little Village Magazine, and Earthwords. In his spare time, he raises his daughter, gardens, and hikes the forests of Iowa.

Contributors

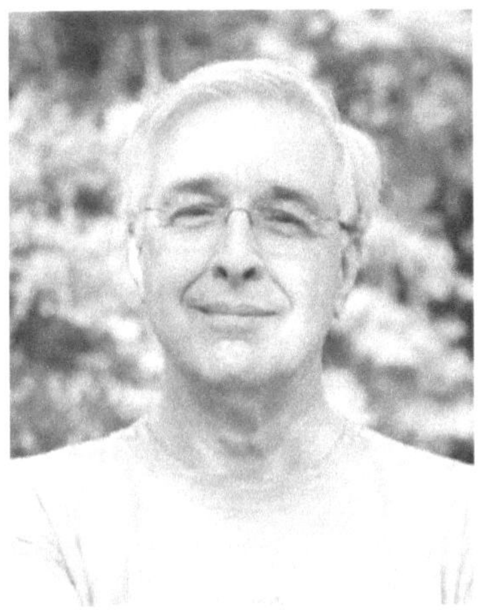

Dennis Maulsby's (he/him) poems and short stories have appeared in numerous journals and on National Public Radio. His traditionally published works include two books of short stories, a collection of short stories and poetry, and a novel. Website: www.dennismaulsby.com.

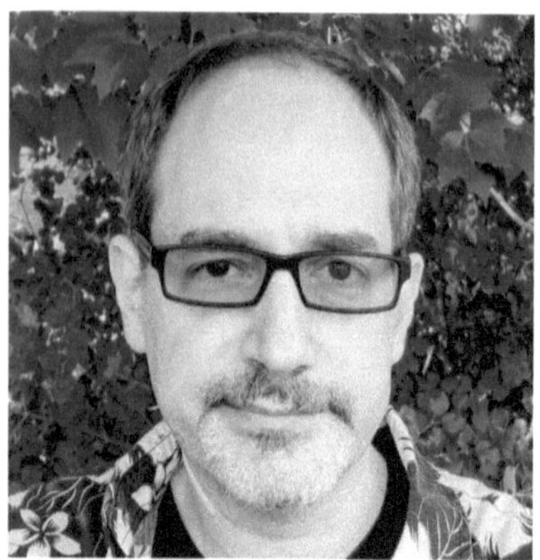

Theodore Michelet Sterling's (he/him) first published story appeared in the anthology Writers of the Flame. Meanwhile, he has worked on a comedic fantasy series for (too many) years that may eventually see the light of day. He lives in Iowa with his wife, two sons, and an indeterminate number of cats (usually three).

Contributors

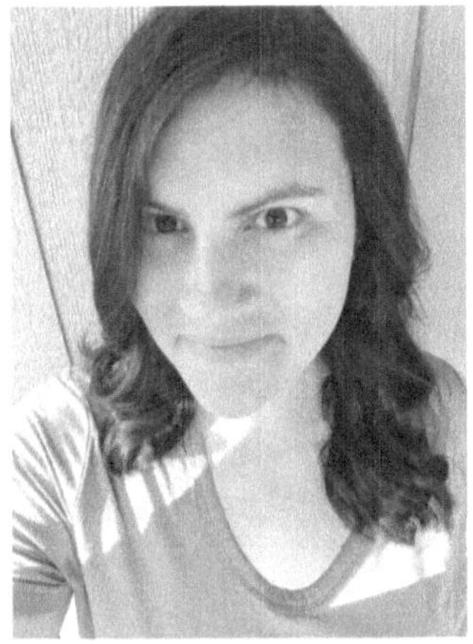

Kristel Saxton (she/her My work emphasizes & explores design elements such as line, shape, contrast & texture. They ask viewers to attend to the sensual aspects of visual experience. The subject matter itself is secondary, although not unimportant. I find hidden meaning & connection in the worlds between & within subjects.

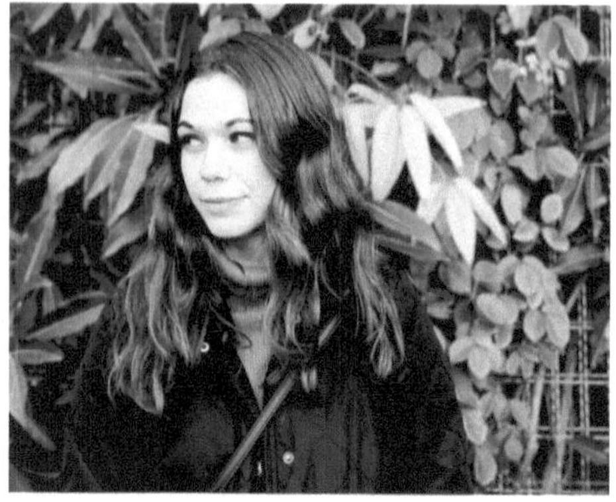

Rachel Schneberger (she/her) is a software
application developer based in Iowa City, Iowa.
Having degrees in both computer science and
music performance, Rachel is drawn to creative
outlets. As a curious, novice writer, she enjoys
traveling, reading, and taking leisurely strolls
through the cemetery with her dog.

Acknowledgments

We want to give our heartfelt thanks to everyone listed below. The Writers' Rooms ran an Indiegogo campaign to raise funds in order to print this anthology, and these lovely people contributed to its success. Without their generosity, you wouldn't be holding this book in your hands today. Thank you for helping us elevate Iowan voices!

Nicholas Lee

Emma Staff

Jill Cronbaugh

Matthew Friberg

Heather Blatt

Joe Altmaier

Brenna Deutchman

Roger Randolph

Sean Finn

Rachael Weber

Jorie Slodki

Sryjones

Jennifer Patterson

and help all writers with their craft. We strive to encourage and foster community-based knowledge to help lead literary sessions and provide a safe, positive writing environment. Our Rooms are moderated by both our Concierges and the members of our community. Community-led sessions tap into the wealth of our collective knowledge, allowing our writers to both share their own experiences and learn from other attendees.

The Rooms can't exist without you and your passion and experience!

OUR PEOPLE

Concierge members come from the writing community. All of our current concierges were interested in their topics and became knowledgeable about their genre through reading, writing, and taking lessons of their own. Anyone interested in leading a particular genre- or topic-based Room is welcome to e-mail us at

welcome@thewritersrooms.org.

The rest of the Room membership comes from eager writer minds who want to know more about a particular genre or topic. Some have even graciously led lessons for us. We're always looking for more people to share their expertise.

Find out more at: Facebook (IAWritersRooms),

and follow us on Instagram (@WritersRooms)

and Twitter (@IAWritersRooms).

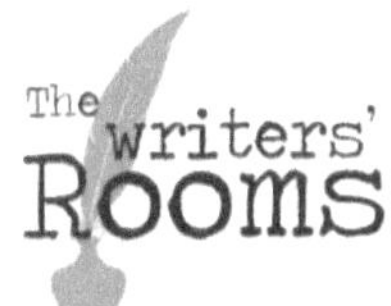

Support The Writers' Rooms!

We are Writers Helping Writers

The Writers' Rooms are and will always be free to the public.
Everything we do is out-of-pocket from our Director and Concierges, funded by the sale of anthologies and merchandise, or the product of generous donations from the community.
All proceeds are used wholly for The Writers' Rooms' day-to-day operational expenses, to fund event appearances and community outreach, and to publish our annual Community Anthology.

Donate through...
PayPal! Paypal.me/thewritersrooms
CashApp! Cash.app/$thewritersrooms
Ko-fi! Ko-fi.com/thewritersrooms

Purchase our Anthologies!
thewritersrooms.org/store
Prefer eBooks? <u>A New Adventure</u>, <u>Writers of the Depths</u>, <u>Writers of the Aether</u> *and* <u>Writers</u>

<u>of the Flame</u> *are available for purchase on our website.*

Check out our Teespring! the-writers-rooms.creator-spring.com
Here you can buy a host of different items from The Writers' Rooms and specific Rooms, like our **TWR Pride shirt** *or* **Make It Gay mug***! Not seeing something you want? Submit a request to welcome@thewritersrooms.org!*

Subscribe to our Patreon! www.patreon.com/TheWritersRooms
This subscription service allows you to support The Writers' Rooms on a monthly basis, for as little as $1 per month. You will be featured on our Donate page at www.thewritersrooms.org/donate. Keep an eye out for more Patron perks soon!

Thank you!
We can't do this without you!